BUILDING
Healthy Corridors

TRANSFORMING **URBAN AND SUBURBAN ARTERIALS** INTO
THRIVING PLACES

Urban Land Institute | Building Healthy Places Initiative

The Rose Center FOR PUBLIC LEADERSHIP | **NLC** NATIONAL LEAGUE OF CITIES

COVER IMAGES, CLOCKWISE FROM TOP:

A bus rapid transit system in Cleveland has improved connectivity and stimulated development along Euclid Avenue. *(Craig Kuhner)* | Safe bicycle infrastructure can decrease injuries and encourage cycling. *(Rachel MacCleery)* | Wide sidewalks, buffered from travel lanes, are critical to keep pedestrians, bicyclists, and other users safe. *(Craig Kuhner)* | Celebrating the culture of the community can help define an identity for the corridor and attract visitors. *(ULI Los Angeles)*

Recommended bibliographical listing:
Urban Land Institute. *Building Healthy Corridors: Transforming Urban and Suburban Arterials into Thriving Places.* Washington, D.C.: Urban Land Institute, 2016.

ISBN: 978-0-87420-393-6

About the Urban Land Institute

The Urban Land Institute is a nonprofit research and education organization whose mission is to provide leadership in the responsible use of land and in creating and sustaining thriving communities world-wide. Established in 1936, the Institute today has more than 39,000 members and associates from 82 countries, representing the entire spectrum of the land use and development disciplines. ULI relies heavily on the experience of its members. It is through member involvement and information resources that ULI has been able to set standards of excellence in development practice. The Institute is recognized internationally as one of America's most respected and widely quoted sources of objective information on urban planning, growth, and development.

About the Building Healthy Places Initiative

Around the world, communities are working to become healthier. Through the Building Healthy Places Initiative, launched in summer 2013, ULI is leveraging the power of its global networks to shape projects and places in ways that improve the health of people and communities. Learn more about and connect with the Building Healthy Places Initiative at www.uli.org/health.

About the Rose Center for Public Leadership in Land Use

The Rose Center for Public Leadership in Land Use encourages and supports excellence in land use decision making by local governments. A program of the National League of Cities in partnership with ULI, the Rose Center seeks to foster creative, efficient, practical, and sustainable land use policies by providing public officials with access to information, best practices, peer networks, and other resources.

The flagship program of the Rose Center is the Daniel Rose Fellowship, which provides city leaders with the insights, peer-to-peer learning, and analysis they need to improve their cities. The Rose Center also hosts workshops, forums, and webinars on various aspects of community building in cities across the country.

About This Report

Building Healthy Corridors: Transforming Urban and Suburban Arterials into Thriving Places explores strategies for transforming commercial corridors—found in nearly every community across the United States—into places that support the health of the people who live, work, and travel along them. This report is the result of a two-year project that involved partnerships with four communities in the United States that are working to improve a specific corridor in ways that positively affect health. This report serves as a resource and reference for those who are undertaking corridor redevelopment efforts; it highlights the importance of health in decision-making processes; and it provides guidance, strategies, and insights for reworking corridors in health-promoting ways.

ULI is grateful to the **Robert Wood Johnson Foundation**, the **Colorado Health Foundation**, and the **ULI Foundation** for their support of this project and the Building Healthy Places Initiative.

ULI Senior Executives

Patrick L. Phillips
Global Chief Executive Officer

Michael Terseck
Chief Financial Officer/
Chief Administrative Officer

Cheryl Cummins
Global Governance Officer

Jeanne R. Myerson
Chief Executive Officer, ULI Americas

Lisette van Doorn
Chief Executive Officer, ULI Europe

John Fitzgerald
Chief Executive Officer, ULI Asia Pacific

Kathleen B. Carey
President and Chief Executive Officer,
ULI Foundation

Adam Smolyar
Chief Marketing and Membership Officer

Steve Ridd
Executive Vice President, Global Business
Operations

Stephanie Wasser
Executive Vice President, Member Networks

Primary Author

Sara Hammerschmidt
Senior Director, Content

Contributing Authors

Aysha Cohen
Senior Associate, Content

Grant Hayes
Research Assistant

Report Staff

Kathleen B. Carey
President and Chief Executive Officer,
ULI Foundation
(as Chief Content Officer)

Rachel MacCleery
Senior Vice President, Content

Jess Zimbabwe
Director of Urban Development,
National League of Cities

Gideon Berger
Program Director, Daniel Rose Fellowship Program,
National League of Cities

Matt Norris
Senior Associate, Content

James A. Mulligan
Senior Editor

Sarah Umberger, Publications Professionals LLC
Manuscript Editor

Betsy Van Buskirk
Creative Director

John Hall Design Group
Designer

Craig Chapman
Senior Director, Publishing Operations

ULI District Council Staff

Rose Faeges-Easton
Senior Director, ULI Nashville
Nashville, Tennessee

Gail Goldberg
Executive Director, ULI Los Angeles
Los Angeles, California

Diane Kushlan
Coordinator, ULI Idaho
Boise, Idaho

Michael Leccese
Executive Director, ULI Colorado
Denver, Colorado

Jonathan Nettler
Senior Director, ULI Los Angeles
Los Angeles, California

Contents

Introduction

THE HEALTHY CORRIDOR OPPORTUNITY

Across the United States, cities are looking for ways to become more attractive to investors, competitive for new businesses, livable for residents, and exciting to visitors. They aspire to be vibrant, equitable, and sustainable places, with a mix of uses and a variety of transportation options.

However, nearly every community across the country is challenged by the presence of automobile-centric commercial corridors. These corridors are characterized by the following:

» a wide road with multiple lanes;

» high-speed traffic;

» nonexistent or limited transit service;

» buildings separated from the street by large parking lots;

» unsightly utility poles and wires;

» a lack of trees and vegetation; and

» sidewalks that are narrow, in poor condition, interrupted with driveway curb cuts, and unbuffered from the travel lanes—if they exist at all.

These adverse conditions negatively affect people who live, work, and travel along and rely on commercial corridors for services and amenities to meet their daily needs. However, corridors are also essential for local and regional trips and often serve as major connectors. As a result, they often suffer from high traffic volumes and congestion, which make them unappealing and unsafe for all users, including drivers.

Redevelopment through infrastructure improvements, new site developments, and aesthetic enhancements has made a difference to the physical conditions along some corridors. The *Urban Street Design*

Guide, published in 2013 by the National Association of City Transportation Officials, provides schematics and strategies for enhancing the design of multiple types of roadways to accommodate a variety of users.

ULI has embarked on many corridor studies over the past two decades as well. *Ten Principles for Reinventing America's Suburban Strips*, published in 2001, lays out a set of recommendations for reversing the low-density, automobile-oriented development trends plaguing suburban commercial strips. The ten principles—which include "ignite leadership and nurture partnership," "establish pulse nodes of development," and "create the place"—can be applied to urban, suburban, and rural corridors alike.

In addition, more than 12 Technical Assistance Program panels, which are run through ULI's district councils, and another 13 urban redevelopment challenges selected by cities participating in the Daniel Rose Fellowship program (a joint program of ULI and the National League of Cities) have focused on corridor redevelopment.

Commuting percentages by mode

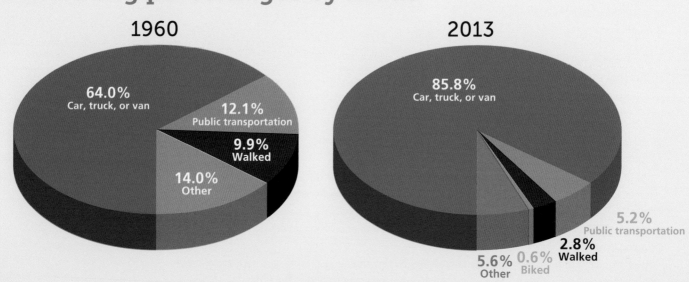

1960

- 64.0% Car, truck, or van
- 12.1% Public transportation
- 9.9% Walked
- 14.0% Other

2013

- 85.8% Car, truck, or van
- 5.2% Public transportation
- 2.8% Walked
- 0.6% Biked
- 5.6% Other

Sources: U.S. Census Bureau, Decennial Census for 1960 and American Community Survey for 2013.

Although reinventing the street, sidewalk, and adjacent properties along corridors has received a lot of attention, less consideration has been paid to restructuring the corridors—in conjunction with improving access from nearby neighborhoods—in ways that might improve health outcomes for residents, workers, and visitors. The rise of chronic diseases such as obesity, heart disease, diabetes, and asthma that are partially attributable to the built environment, as well as the rise of injury rates for pedestrians and bicyclists, points to the need to look more holistically at how corridor redevelopment can create the opportunity to foster healthier behavior and lifestyles.

Over the past several decades, commuting and other trips by car have increased, while walking, biking, and public transit use have decreased overall. The percentage of work trips taken by automobile has increased from 64 percent in 1960 to nearly 90 percent in 2013, although bike commuting (still a small fraction compared with commuting by car) is currently the fastest-growing mode of travel to work. Conversely, the percentage of school-aged children who walked or biked to school decreased from 40 percent in 1969 to just 13 percent in 2009. The design of the built environment has contributed to those trends.

From a safety perspective, people may feel safer as drivers or passengers inside vehicles than as pedestrians or cyclists—and with good reason, particularly on streets without sidewalks or bike lanes. Pedestrians on streets without sidewalks are 200 percent more likely to be involved in crashes than pedestrians on streets with sidewalks. Vehicle speeds contribute to fatalities: for pedestrians, the average risk of death increases as speed increases, from 10 percent at an impact speed of 23 miles per hour to 50 percent at 42 miles per hour. Measures that slow vehicle speed can reduce the number of automobile crashes that cause injuries by 10 percent on main roads and by 25 percent on residential streets.

Just as urban waterfront redevelopment capitalizes on public space in cities, commercial corridors should be considered assets that can be redeveloped to support civic life, enhance economic development, and serve as neighborhood resources.

The American public wants redevelopment that promotes healthier living. Fifty percent of those surveyed by ULI in 2015 reported that walkability is a priority when considering where to live. Similarly, 52 percent would like to live in a place where they do not have to use a car very often.

ABOVE: Typical land uses along commercial corridors include used-car lots, fast-food restaurants, and other uses that do not serve the daily needs of residents. *(Guy Hand)*
OPPOSITE: Poorly maintained sidewalks coupled with undesirable land uses discourage pedestrian activity and incentivize driving. *(Courtesy of Sasaki)*

Automobile-centric corridors often divide neighborhoods and interrupt social cohesion because they are unsafe to cross. The neighborhoods most affected tend to be lower-income neighborhoods whose residents are not well served by the plethora of car sales lots and fast-food restaurants lining these corridors. In addition, certain corridor land uses, such as gas stations, may cause environmental problems.

These complex issues need to be addressed by engaging residents and advocacy groups to identify the economic and environmental problems along corridors; an improvement plan can then be formulated to benefit all. Creating corridors that support a variety of daily needs—such as allowing people to walk or bike safely to purchase groceries, run other errands, or exercise—is critical to creating a healthy community.

The Healthy Corridors Approach

Corridor redevelopment is not a new topic. Various planning and design approaches—such as complete streets, living streets, and great streets—aim to redevelop commercial corridors to meet more of their users' needs, including their need for walking and biking rather than just traveling by car. But a marked difference between a healthy corridors approach and other approaches is that the former considers how the street supports the daily needs and affects the **health** of all who live, work, and travel along it.

The **healthy corridors approach** considers how the corridor contributes to the overall health of the surrounding community, including supplying opportunities to be physically active. It also considers safety, housing affordability, transportation options, environmental sustainability, and social cohesion, as well as modifications that would link residents to the corridor and improve connections to jobs and other parts of the community.

Understanding a wide range of baseline factors, including the demographics of communities surrounding the corridor, current transit access, market conditions, types of land uses and businesses, and community needs and interests—as well as sidewalk, travel lane, intersection, and other infrastructure conditions—is the foundation of this approach.

Health Impact Assessments

A Health Impact Assessment (HIA) is an evidence-based process that engages the community, gathers health-related information, and identifies strategies to improve community and individual health. Used to identify potential health impacts of projects, plans, and policies, HIAs consist of six phases typically used in other types of impact assessment: screening, scoping, assessment, recommendations, reporting, and evaluation and monitoring.

The healthy corridors approach takes into account the needs of surrounding neighborhoods. Doing so is particularly important if the surrounding neighborhoods contain residents who are low-income or excluded from decision-making processes.

A process that can foster the incorporation of both health and equity into community planning and engagement efforts is a Health Impact Assessment (HIA). In Minnesota, the city of St. Paul used an HIA when developing a new plan for the area around University Avenue; the plan incorporated a new rail line connecting the downtowns of Minneapolis and St. Paul. Through the HIA process, which was led by health- and equity-focused community organizations, community members of the racially and ethnically diverse high-poverty area became engaged in the city's rezoning process.

Those who examine commercial corridors often see that roads need to be reconfigured to improve pedestrian, bicyclist, and vehicle safety; but to create a complete revitalization plan, they must also consider people-focused outcomes other than safety. Using health as the defining criterion for corridor redevelopment—or for any type of land use project—can provide a new way of looking at problems and potential solutions. The health lens allows diverse stakeholders, such as public health professionals, local hospital systems, and health-focused nonprofits and foundations, to engage in the process.

By broadening the conversation and the focus to include not only an emphasis on pedestrian and bicyclist safety but also on access to healthy food, physical activity opportunities, economic opportunities, enhanced connections to other parts of the city, and a variety of housing options, local governments, businesses, residents, and other stakeholders can create a more holistically healthy corridor. To ensure that improvements will benefit everyone, it is also critical to prevent resident displacement by retaining and providing affordable housing, including market-rate affordable housing, and by developing strategies to retain local businesses. Engaging a wide spectrum of stakeholders—including residents, advocacy organizations, and social justice groups—around the concept of healthy corridor redevelopment can help embed a culture of health within the community and beyond.

Healthy Corridor Typology

A primary activity of ULI's Healthy Corridors project was to define a healthy corridor and identify the components that make up a holistically healthy corridor and its surrounding area. A healthy corridor has land uses and services that allow residents and visitors to make healthy lifestyle choices more easily. A healthy corridor is a place that reflects the culture of the community, promotes social cohesion, inspires and facilitates healthy eating and active living, provides and connects to a variety of economic and educational opportunities and housing and transportation choices, and adapts to the needs and concerns of residents.

Improved infrastructure	» Frequent, safe, and well-marked pedestrian crossings
	» Safe and well-marked bike lanes
	» Traffic speeds that accommodate pedestrians, bicyclists, and other users
	» Reduced traffic congestion
	» Utility lines and traffic signs and signals that are underground or that blend in
	» Sidewalks that link adjacent neighborhoods to the corridor and that are unobstructed, wide enough for a variety of users, and buffered from the street
	» Streetscapes that include amenities for visual interest and safety, including seating, trees for shade, and green buffers
	» Lighting that improves visibility and safety for pedestrians and bicyclists
	» Features that improve accessibility for all types of users, in compliance with Americans with Disabilities Act standards
Design and land use patterns that support community needs	» Vibrant retail environment
	» Housing options for all income levels
	» Buildings adjacent or proximate to sidewalks
	» Improved parking strategies and shared parking
	» High-quality parks and public spaces
	» Healthy food options
Engaged and supported people who live, work, and travel along the corridor	» Engaged residents and local business owners
	» Organizations that facilitate long-term improvements and resident engagement
	» Regular programs in community gathering spaces
	» Accommodations for pets
	» Accommodations for vulnerable populations, including children, the elderly, and people with disabilities
	» A defined identity, drawing on the arts and culture of the community and supported by creative placemaking programming
	» Measures to address safety and perceptions of safety
Linkages to other parts of the city	» Well-connected, multimodal street networks
	» Safe and easily identifiable connections, including sidewalks and trails
	» Transit, including enhanced bus service or rail
	» Bike infrastructure on or adjacent to the corridor

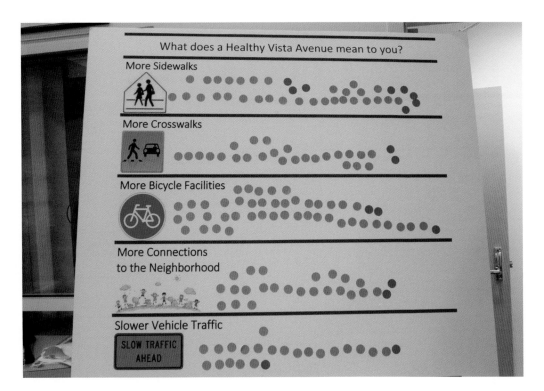

Report Overview

Through strong partnerships among both typical and new stakeholders, corridors across the United States can be redeveloped in ways that create healthier conditions for those who live, work, and travel along them. Through corridor revitalization that is focused on health, communities can become more economically vibrant, equitable, sustainable, and attractive places. The healthy corridors approach helps all involved in corridor redevelopment and community revitalization—the public sector, the private sector, nonprofits, and neighborhood advocacy groups—work together to create a better future.

This summary report presents the results of ULI's two-year Healthy Corridors project, which was undertaken in partnership with the ULI district councils and stakeholders of four corridors in four cities in different parts of the country—Federal Boulevard in Denver, Colorado; Vista Avenue in Boise, Idaho; Van Nuys Boulevard in Los Angeles, California; and Charlotte Avenue in Nashville, Tennessee. Together, these constitute the project's "demonstration corridors." This report is intended to serve as a resource and reference for those who are undertaking corridor redevelopment projects; it highlights the importance of including health factors in decision-making processes, and it provides guidance on how to prioritize the health of those who live, work, and travel along these corridors.

Building on previous ULI Building Healthy Places Initiative publications—including *Ten Principles for Building Healthy Places, Building Healthy Places Toolkit: Strategies for Enhancing Health in the Built Environment,* and *Active Transportation and Real Estate: The Next Frontier*—this report provides a foundation for the real estate and land use communities to understand how to design and construct projects focused on health.

Partnerships are necessary to solve problems within commercial corridors; therefore, this report is targeted to a variety of audiences, including real estate developers, community planners, public and elected officials, public health professionals, transportation professionals, nonprofit leaders, and community decision makers.

This report defines what constitutes a healthy corridor, shares a healthy corridor typology, explores case studies from corridor redevelopment projects across the United States, and summarizes lessons from the project's demonstration corridors. It uses findings to demonstrate specific aspects of a healthy corridor and to outline a process roadmap for transforming commercial corridors into healthier places.

Other helpful materials developed as a part of this project—including sample workshop agendas, a Healthy Corridor Audit Tool, and a resource and strategy guide for corridor redevelopment—can be found at uli.org/healthycorridors.

2 Reinventing Corridors

PROJECT PROFILES

Over the course of the Healthy Corridors project, ULI worked with four corridors to imagine a healthier future. ULI also researched successful corridor redevelopment efforts across the country.

ABOVE: A healthy corridor has improved infrastructure, such as safe and well-marked bike lanes. *(Elvert Barnes/flickr)*

To help determine how to redevelop corridors in ways that promote health, four ULI district councils that were selected through a competitive application process identified problematic corridor sections to study over the course of the Healthy Corridors project, from late 2014 through 2016. These corridor sections served as demonstration corridors for the project. ULI also profiled commercial corridors from across the country—corridors that worked to reinvent themselves.

Reimagining Corridors for the Better

Discussing commercial corridors in the context of public health is a new approach that requires new partnerships and a new way of looking at corridor redevelopment, one that goes beyond economic development opportunities or complete streets. Although there may not yet be an example of a redeveloped corridor that is holistically healthy—that is, a corridor characterized by improved infrastructure; design and land use patterns that support community needs; engaged and supported people who live, work, and travel along the corridor; and linkages to other parts of the city—many cities have successfully implemented components of this healthy corridor typology in an effort to create better corridors.

The following case studies of redeveloped corridors across the United States outline the completed processes and projects that leveraged transportation, design, zoning, community engagement, health, public art, or a combination of these components, to transform corridors and improve conditions for all. The case studies are intended to inspire changes that positively affect health in other corridors across the country, including ULI's demonstration corridors. They show how improvements in infrastructure, housing, sustainability, and cultural amenities along commercial corridors can contribute to creating more vibrant, livable, and healthier places.

The four demonstration corridors participating in ULI's Healthy Corridors project—Federal Boulevard in Denver, Colorado; Vista Avenue in Boise, Idaho; Van Nuys Boulevard in Los Angeles, California; and Charlotte Avenue in Nashville, Tennessee—are striving to become healthy corridors. Their stakeholders are adopting many healthy corridor characteristics in their redevelopment goals, processes, and plans, all of which are designed to consider health in a comprehensive way. These are discussed further in Chapter 3.

Further information and resources regarding the strategies undertaken by the cities highlighted in the following case studies—and the strategies planned by the demonstration corridors—are explored in the companion piece, "Building Healthy Corridors: Strategy and Resource Guide," which can be downloaded at uli.org/healthycorridors.

Strategy and Resource Guide

A companion piece to this report, the "Strategy and Resource Guide," provides a menu of opportunities for focusing on health within redevelopment efforts. The guide is intended to serve as a resource for communities interested in redeveloping commercial strip corridors in partnership with regional and community stakeholders. To download the guide, visit uli.org/healthycorridors.

Many communities have integrated elements of a healthy corridor into their redevelopment plans. (Craig Kuhner)

Columbia Pike
Arlington County, Virginia

Using Form-Based Codes to Improve Design and Land Use Patterns

Redevelopment Strategies

» Form-based codes (FBCs)
» Tax increment financing

Results and Lessons Learned

» Although implementing an FBC is a lengthy process, it can help incentivize developers to redevelop in ways that improve the streetscape, density, and land uses of a corridor.

» In Arlington County, the use of FBCs has been instrumental both in preserving existing affordable housing and in encouraging new affordable housing.

» Other critical infrastructure improvements include utilities moved underground; relocated parking, bike, and pedestrian amenities; and enhanced transit services.

LEFT: Before, Columbia Pike had narrow sidewalks and an automobile-oriented streetscape. *(Arlington County)*
ABOVE: A form-based code has helped transform Columbia Pike into a safer and more pedestrian-friendly arterial. *(Arlington County)*

Located outside Washington, D.C., in Arlington County, Virginia, Columbia Pike is a thoroughfare stretching more than three miles—from the edge of the Pentagon to the border of Fairfax County. The road was built in 1810 to connect Washington's Long Bridge to the Little River Turnpike and the rest of Virginia. It evolved to become an automobile-oriented arterial—lined with fast-food restaurants, drive-through restaurants and banks, convenience stores, and strip malls—characterized by intense traffic congestion.

Arlington County sought to alleviate the congestion through the Columbia Pike Initiative, a corridor revitalization plan focused on the commercial corridors and adopted in 2002. The initiative was organized around an innovative Commercial Centers Form-Based Code (FBC) and supportive government-led programs, including a partnership with D.C.'s Metrobus. In 2008, the Arlington County Board issued a charge to begin

work on Phase II of the Columbia Pike Initiative, which focused on multifamily residential areas located between the commercial centers. Phase II culminated in the adoption of the Neighborhoods Area Plan in 2012, which outlined the goals and tools that could be used to create the transportation, form, and housing vision for the multifamily areas. In 2013, the Columbia Pike Neighborhoods Form-Based Code (NFBC) was adopted in support of this vision. Together, the plans and the two codes work to create more urban parks and affordable housing, promote a safe biking and walking environment, and improve the corridor's transit options.

The two form-based codes were designed to kick-start development along Columbia Pike. The preapproved standards act as an incentive for developers because they allow for a much faster approval process, saving developers both time and money. Developers who choose to use the FBCs can get project approvals typically within six to nine months with only one or two public hearings, whereas the conventional process can take nine to 12 months or even longer. Each code includes a process for administrative approval by the zoning administrator for smaller and less complex projects.

Within the FBCs are prescriptions for street planning and standards for building envelopes, streetscapes, and architecture. In the Commercial Centers FBC, buildings are required to have street frontage, first-floor retail space, and built-in bicycle amenities.

Affordable housing development is incentivized through the NFBC, which requires that 20 to 35 percent of net new units in developments be affordable to residents with incomes of up to 60 percent of the area median income for a period of 30 years.

To help meet the ambitious affordable housing goal, the county also employed financial tools. The Transit-Oriented Affordable Housing (TOAH) Fund was adopted by the county in 2013. Affordable housing developers who apply for low-income housing tax credits may put TOAH funds toward infrastructure-related items (such as underground utilities, tree preservation, and streetscape improvements) and county fees (such as a certificate of occupancy, building permits, and utility fees) to help keep project costs under the Virginia Housing and Development Authority total development cost limits and increase competitiveness for tax credits.

The Columbia Pike Tax Increment Financing (TIF) Area was established as a funding mechanism for the TOAH. The Columbia Pike TIF dedicates 25 percent of incremental new tax revenue generated by new development and property appreciation within specifically designated commercial and multifamily residential revitalization districts to affordable housing along the corridor.

Arlington County's commitment to affordable housing has been enhanced through the NFBC. Other tools such as the Affordable Housing Investment Fund (AHIF) and low-income housing tax credits have helped with the preservation and creation of new units. The county has preserved or created 938 affordable units along the Pike since 2012. These units were preserved or created using AHIF, public/private partnerships, or the affordable housing requirements under the NFBC. Of the total 938 affordable units, 499 were preserved in the existing buildings with assistance from AHIF loans or the NFBC affordable housing requirements.

Because of the FBCs and programming planned by Arlington County, Columbia Pike now has elements that make it a healthier and more pedestrian-friendly area. Since the FBC's adoption, the corridor has added more than 1 million square feet of commercial space, a new community center, a weekly farmers market, a supermarket, about 3,000 residential units, and multiple open spaces that complement a nearby 45-mile paved walking, running, and bike trail. The county is building new bike and pedestrian infrastructure, and the FBC mandates that all parking must be behind or underneath buildings to preserve and enhance the streetscape. As a requirement of the code, any redevelopment project must also finance the burial of utilities on that block.

Columbia Pike is now the busiest bus transit corridor in Virginia, with bus lines that have increased ridership and frequency and that connect to the Pentagon Metro station. The corridor also features two walking loops, "bike boulevards" on adjacent streets, bike racks, and six Capital Bikeshare stations.

Form-Based Codes

A form-based code (FBC) is a regulation, not a guideline. As such, it is a means of regulating land development to achieve a specific urban form and to create a destination in an area. Unlike traditional zoning, which is based on separation of uses, FBCs use physical form as the organizing principle of design and development to create a high-quality public realm. An FBC is adopted into city, town, or county law and is a powerful alternative to conventional zoning regulations. Benefits to developers include faster-than-normal approval of their plans, a lower risk of residents opposing the project, and a potential for increasing the density of the project.

LEFT: Before the form-based code, strip malls and other developments along Columbia Pike catered to drivers. *(Courtesy of BM Smith).*
BELOW: Parking relocated from the front to the back of developments helps create a better environment for pedestrians and bicyclists. *(Arlington County)*

Aurora Avenue North
Shoreline, Washington

A Better Corridor through Infrastructure Investment

Redevelopment Strategies

» Broad infrastructure improvements focused on alternative transportation modes

» Creative financing, using a mix of 21 funding sources

Results and Lessons Learned

» Perseverance pays off: the project took nearly 20 years to complete, but the corridor is now a much safer, healthier, and more connected place.

» Numerous improvements to infrastructure along the corridor—including sidewalks, medians, lighting, and utilities placed underground—have made the corridor a safer and more attractive place for biking and walking.

» A new bus rapid transit (BRT) service has increased transportation options for residents who live in housing adjacent to the corridor.

RIGHT: Before reconstruction, the Aurora Avenue North corridor was unsightly and automobile-oriented and lacked pedestrian amenities. *(City of Shoreline)*

ABOVE: The removal of aboveground utility lines and the introduction of medians, greenery, crosswalks, street and traffic lights, and sidewalks have greatly enhanced the corridor's aesthetics, functionality, and safety. *(City of Shoreline)*

The first-tier suburban city of Shoreline, just north of Seattle, began its ambitious redevelopment of the heavily used Aurora Avenue North corridor just three years after the city's incorporation in 1995. Before reconstruction, Aurora Avenue North was an automobile-centric highway featuring gas stations, shopping centers, convenience stores, adult clubs, and tobacco and alcohol stores. The four-lane road had an average of 40,000 to 45,000 vehicles and 7,000 bus riders per day and one of the highest crash rates in the state, at nearly one per day and one fatality per year.

The city knew that the redevelopment of Aurora would take a long-term commitment, and for the next 18 years, Shoreline worked to address land use and safety issues and to improve the conditions of the corridor and the surrounding neighborhoods. The three-mile project was completed without debt

in 2016 using a mix of 21 different funding sources, including Shoreline's capital improvement program as well as county, state, and federal funding.[1]

After reaching consensus on elements of a unified vision using design studies and public input in 1998, the city of Shoreline sought to achieve the vision by improving safety, spurring economic development, alleviating traffic congestion, enhancing sustainability, and increasing the number of amenities for pedestrians. To accomplish these goals, the city landscaped medians, added left- and U-turn pockets, upgraded sidewalks and pedestrian amenities, colored and scored concrete crosswalks, and incorporated new street and pedestrian lighting.

Shoreline improved the street appearance and upgraded the capacity of the utility infrastructure by moving it underground—an expensive and complex undertaking that required collaboration with many partners. The city installed sustainable stormwater features and living retaining walls and developed a rainwater filtration plaza for pedestrians.

As part of the project, Shoreline improved its three-mile section of the Interurban Trail—a 24-mile trail connecting the cities of Seattle and Everett—to make it a seamless cycling trail with iconic bridge crossings over Aurora Avenue North and North 155th Street.

To improve transit options, a new dedicated bus rapid transit (BRT) service called RapidRide, the fifth of six county BRT lines, was developed with the help of state and federal resources in partnership with the King County Department of Transportation's Metro Transit division and the city of Seattle. To support the service, Shoreline established what it calls "business-access transit lanes," which support access to businesses and also provide stopping spaces for buses; installed an intelligent fiber-based transportation system to enable buses to communicate with traffic signals; and incorporated preboarding payment stations. The prepayment system allows riders to quickly board the buses, which feature low floors, three doors, and "next stop" displays and audio. The corridor's improved bus stops feature electronic next-arrival signs, weather protection coverings, and interior and exterior lighting to improve bus stop visibility.

Since the construction project began in 2005, Shoreline has begun to experience returns on the $146-million investment. Before the project was even complete, crashes declined by 60 percent. Since 2015, Shoreline's Aurora Avenue North has welcomed multiple new businesses and community services: two health clinics, a YMCA, a biotech lab, a Trader Joe's, the City Hall, and a high school. Seven hundred completed housing units span the affordability range, with another 1,000 units either under construction or in the permitting process.

In addition, the Puget Sound Regional Council, the region's planning agency, gave the city

its Vision 2020 Award, and the Federal Highway Administration and the Washington State Department of Transportation presented the city with a 2008 Award of Excellence for Best City Project.

Aurora Avenue North is now Shoreline's main street. It is aesthetically pleasing, safer, more efficient, and optimized for new economic development. The project has improved pedestrian safety, automobile capacity, transit performance, traffic flow, and stormwater management. The BRT is expected to save motorists between $2,000 and $8,000 a year, and, since launching in 2014, bus reliability has improved and weekly ridership has increased by 13 percent. Local leaders foresee that the city's investment will encourage local landowners to redevelop their properties along Aurora and that additional redevelopment could further enhance the corridor for all users.

LEFT: Shoreline's corridor improvements include the addition of a bridge to improve connections along the Interurban Trail, a 24-mile cycling trail between the cities of Seattle and Everett. *(HDR Engineering Inc.)*
BELOW RIGHT: Previously, little emphasis was placed on bus accessibility and passenger comfort along the Aurora corridor. *(City of Shoreline)*
BELOW LEFT: Now, dedicated bus lanes, covered and prominent bus stops, and other bus infrastructure improvements have helped improve BRT reliability and ridership along the Aurora corridor. *(City of Shoreline)*

[1] For the last stretch of corridor improvements, funding sources included the Federal Highway Administration, Washington State Transportation Improvement Board, Washington State Department of Transportation Regional Mobility grants, Washington State Department of Ecology, King County Metro, Seattle City Light, Seattle Public Utilities, Ronald Wastewater District, and the city of Shoreline.

Euclid Avenue
Cleveland, Ohio

Enhancing a Corridor through Transit Investment

Redevelopment Strategies

» Broad infrastructure improvements centered around transit

» Public/private partnerships to fund and implement the project

Results and Lessons Learned

» Strong public/private partnerships between multiple stakeholders contributed to the success of the project.

» The establishment of a new transit line resulted in $6.3 billion in new development, 13,000 new jobs, and more than 4,000 new residential units along the corridor.

Euclid Avenue in Cleveland is celebrated in the city's history as the turn-of-the-20th-century home to John D. Rockefeller and other prominent American businessmen. However, as development pressure and Cleveland's population increased, Euclid Avenue's luxury homes gave way to parking lots and shopping centers.

Beginning in the 1970s, local leaders set out to reestablish the corridor as a major transportation and economic development link by implementing a new transit system along the avenue. Seeking to connect the city's two largest commercial districts—downtown and University Circle—Cleveland stakeholders voted to establish a bus rapid transit (BRT) system in 1998. Known as the HealthLine, the BRT has both improved connectivity and attracted new development to the area since its completion in 2008.

In strategic partnerships with state and federal agencies, local stakeholders—including the city of Cleveland, the Cleveland Clinic, University Hospitals, and the Greater Cleveland Regional Transit Authority (Cleveland's regional planning agency)—

completed the project for a total investment cost of $200 million. The three goals guiding the development were to (1) improve service and efficiency for customers, (2) promote economic and community development along and adjacent to the line, and (3) improve quality of life for residents and visitors of the corridor and for area employees.

Today, the 9.2-mile HealthLine services Cleveland's cultural amenities, businesses, medical centers, and the convention center while operating seven days a week, 24 hours a day, along dedicated bus lanes. HealthLine buses and stations are highly efficient because the hybrid vehicles contain GPS communication, multiple doors for boarding, and text and audio communications. The stops feature raised platforms, fare vending machines, station signage, real-time displays, and interactive kiosks.

In anticipation of increased growth along the corridor, $10 million of the total investment was put toward improving sidewalks, bike lanes, and the utility infrastructure. Design improvements along the corridor include lighting, public art,

newly paved surfaces, and 1,500 trees. Adjacent neighborhoods were given distinct identities through varying tree species, lighting patterns, and pavement and bus shelter designs.

Since the HealthLine's completion, new development and increased stakeholder collaboration have greatly improved the aesthetics and the usability of Euclid Avenue. Transit travel times have been reduced from 40 to 28 minutes. In the first year of operation, ridership increased by 48 percent, and between 2008 and 2015, ridership increased 70 percent.

The HealthLine has been credited with having the highest return on investment of any recent U.S. transit project, with $6.3 billion in develop-

ment along the line, 13,000 new jobs, and more than 4,000 new residential units. The hybrid buses have 75 percent better fuel economy, and the new trees are expected to absorb close to 48 pounds of carbon dioxide per year once they reach maturity. After the BRT was completed, travel between destinations along Euclid Avenue became quicker for those traveling by bus or car and safer for those traveling by foot or bike.

Those accomplishments earned the HealthLine the Grand Award from the American Council of Engineering Companies in 2010, the Global Award for Excellence from ULI in 2011, and the title "Best in North America" by the Institute for Transportation and Development Policy in 2013.

OPPOSITE: A new BRT system has helped reestablish Euclid Avenue as a major transportation corridor in Cleveland. *(Craig Kuhner)*
ABOVE RIGHT: Before, Euclid Avenue was a desolate, car-oriented corridor that lacked public and private investment. *(Jason Hellendrung)*
ABOVE LEFT AND BELOW: Now, Euclid Avenue operates as a complete and scenic street. *(Craig Kuhner)*

Short North Arts District
Columbus, Ohio

A New Hub for Arts and Culture

Redevelopment Strategies

» Special improvement district (SID), funded through property assessments of corridor businesses

» A defined identity centered around arts and culture

Results and Lessons Learned

» Local business owners initiated the redevelopment effort and created a business association to spearhead the transformation of the corridor.

» Regular community programs and an emphasis on arts and culture brought renewed attention and visitors to a formerly neglected and unsafe area.

The Short North Arts District, which is centered on High Street, consists of 14 blocks north of downtown Columbus just south of the Ohio State University campus. Once home to neglected buildings, boarded-up windows, and few businesses—and visited frequently by the police—the area once known as the "Near Northside" became known as "Short North" after the Columbus police gave the area that moniker for being just short of the northern boundary of the downtown precinct. Short North underwent a makeover when local artists, historic preservationists, and small businesses began to transform the area into an arts district in the 1980s.

In 1983, the Short North Business Association was founded to access funding and develop the area into a thriving community. One year later, a group of area gallery owners created the Gallery Hop, a monthly event to showcase new art exhibits. That move brought an influx of visitors, residents, and businesses to the area.

By the late 1980s, a group of local residents created a satirical and countercultural annual July Fourth event now known as the Doo Dah Parade. Thirty years later, programming continues and consists of many events concentrated on or near High Street, including the street concert and fashion show "HighBall Halloween"; a weekend-long concert titled the "Community Festival," which features local bands; and the Stonewall Columbus Pride Parade.

In 1999, the Short North Special Improvement District (SID) was created by community leaders to enhance the safety, cleanliness, and beauty of the Short North Arts District. The organization is funded through the collection of property assessments from district businesses, and that funding enables the organization to provide services and public improvements.

In 2012, the Short North Business Association merged with the Short North SID to form the Short North Alliance (SNA), which is contracted annually by the SID. The SNA works to continue the Short North Arts District's development as a vibrant, creative, and inclusive community and arts destination while maintaining the area's position as "the art and soul of Columbus." To accomplish these goals, the SNA has continued to market the area and to serve property and business owners while maintaining the management and scheduling of events.

As programming and an organizational structure have come together, the Short North Arts

District's community health and social connectedness have greatly improved. Today, the Gallery Hop includes restaurants, galleries, and shops, and it attracts more than 25,000 attendees a year. More than 30,000 people participate in HighBall, an estimated 80,000 attend the Community Festival, about 500,000 spectators watch the Pride Parade, and the Doo Dah Parade has become locally renowned. Through the SID, Columbus's tradition of illuminated arches was restored with the installation of 17 steel arches that create an identity for the district.

Those improvements have gained much national attention: the Short North Arts District has been recognized by the *New York Times*, *USA Today*, *Fox News*, and various other media outlets. Moreover, 34 new businesses opened in 2015, and 2.5 million people visited the community the same year. By bringing a variety of groups together, the Short North Arts District has become a more vibrant and livable community.

OPPOSITE TOP: The Short North Arts District has been nationally recognized for its infrastructure and programming improvements. *(Bailey Lytle, Short North Alliance)*
OPPOSITE INSET: Short North's identity has been restored and its social capital boosted by the introduction of programming and a business association. *(Bailey Lytle, Short North Alliance)*
ABOVE: Once known for its crime, Columbus's Short North neighborhood has become a popular cultural destination that attracts over 2 million diverse visitors. *(Top: Bailey Lytle, Short North Alliance. Inset: Dana Bernstein, Short North Alliance)*

Edgewater Drive
Orlando, Florida

A Safer Street through Lane Reduction

Redevelopment Strategies
» State Department of Transportation funding
» Lane reduction to improve pedestrian and bike access and safety

Results and Lessons Learned
» Road reconfigurations such as lane reductions that deemphasize the automobile, as well as reduced vehicle speeds and traffic volumes, make the road safer for all types of users.

» Because of the road restriping, total collisions decreased by 40 percent, and injury rates decreased by 71 percent.

» Slowing traffic and improving the pedestrian and bike experience improved property values and the performance of local businesses along the corridor.

Streets have played a major role in the development of College Park, a neighborhood adjacent to downtown Orlando, Florida. The neighborhood's Princeton, Harvard, and Yale streets influenced the naming of the city's first subdivision and eventually the naming of the neighborhood.

Beginning in 1999, local stakeholders gave College Park a new identity by transforming Edgewater Drive, its main street. The four-lane road was extremely unsafe; it carried more than 20,000 speeding motorists per day, and it experienced crashes nearly every three days and injuries every nine days. Because the road also contained limited space for sidewalks, bike lanes, and streetscape, the city of Orlando implemented a lane reduction—or "road diet"—to regain space for pedestrians and bicyclists.

Since the project's implementation, Edgewater Drive has become a noticeably healthier and safer street. Traffic speeds and the number of crashes

have been reduced, and both the volume and satisfaction of pedestrians and bicyclists have increased.

The project emerged from a neighborhood improvement plan called the Neighborhood Horizon Plan and from anticipation surrounding the resurfacing of Edgewater Drive in 2001. Hoping to maximize the opportunity, the city—in collaboration with neighborhood stakeholders—formulated a vision, set of goals, and plan for the redevelopment of a 1.5-mile stretch of Edgewater between Par Street and Lakeview Street.

The goals emphasized the vision of the corridor as a vibrant, pedestrian-oriented commercial district with reduced incidents of speeding, improved bike and pedestrian infrastructure, and an enhanced streetscape. To achieve the goals, the city and the Florida Department of Transportation (FDOT) negotiated plans for a road diet in conjunction with regularly scheduled maintenance. This approach required removing one vehicle lane

and reconfiguring the road through lane restriping; these changes were funded by FDOT and required the state of Florida to transfer control of the street to the city.

After gaining control of Edgewater Drive, the city of Orlando initiated the project. Before committing to permanent improvements, the city implemented a temporary lane reduction, using tape to restripe the road, and then performed a before-and-after analysis that looked at crash and injury rates, vehicle speeds, traffic volumes, on-street parking, travel times, and bicyclist volumes. The analysis showed that those indicators were improved by the lane reduction, and the tape was replaced with permanent striping in December 2002. Ultimately, the city converted four lanes to three; the road now has one travel lane in each direction and a center, two-way turn lane. The city also added bike lanes in both directions and widened on-street parking.

Because of this project, College Park's main street has become a thriving corridor. Safety greatly improved after the project: total collisions dropped by 40 percent, injury rates declined 71 percent, and traffic counts briefly dropped 12 percent before returning to original levels. Pedestrian counts increased by 23 percent, bicycling activity by 30 percent, and on-street parking—which buffers the sidewalks from automobile traffic—by 41 percent.

In addition, the corridor has gained 77 new businesses and an additional 560 jobs since 2008.

The value of property adjacent to Edgewater and within a half mile of the corridor rose 80 percent and 70 percent, respectively.

Such positive results have gained national attention and satisfied local stakeholders, who made no requests to restore Edgewater to a four-lane road when it was resurfaced in 2012.

Second Street
Rochester, Minnesota

Creating Place with Infrastructure and Streetscape Improvements

Redevelopment Strategies

» Lane reduction to improve pedestrian and bike access and safety

» Creative financing, using a mix of sources to fund the project

Results and Lessons Learned

» A comprehensive place-making plan, including infrastructure and street-scape improvements, made the corridor safer for all types of users.

» Branding the neighbor-hood as the "Uptown District" helped contrib-ute to economic growth and development along the corridor.

» After improvements were made, vehicle speeds along Second Street dropped from between 45 and 50 miles per hour to 30 miles per hour.

The nearly three-mile-long Second Street corridor, which extends from the center of down-town Rochester to West Circle Drive, is the eco-nomic hub of the city, with nearly half of all the city's jobs within walking distance, including the prestigious Mayo Health Clinic. Before the com-pletion of a redevelopment project along Second Street in 2015, the economic energy stopped at the U.S. Highway 52 bridge. West of the bridge, Second Street consisted of seven lanes (including two parking lanes and a center turn lane), and 22,000 high-speed vehicles per day traveled it in peak locations. The way the corridor was designed limited pedestrian and bicycle mobility and contributed to underutilized on-street parking (be-cause of the risks associated with parking adjacent to high-speed vehicles).

To reduce the area's automobile-centric nature and to improve its economic trajectory, the city

and area stakeholders completed an inclusive rede-velopment project in 2015. That project revitalized about 1.5 miles of Second Street between U.S. Highway 52 and West Circle Drive. Later rebranded as the Uptown District, the area has since assumed a new identity as a pedestrian-oriented neighbor-hood that is primed for economic growth.

The $7 million project was initiated by area stakeholders in 2009 with the hope of improving the adjacent neighborhoods. It was completed in 2015 by the city in collaboration with private

contractors, Olmsted County, and the Minnesota Department of Transportation. Stakeholders used multiple funding sources, including federal transportation dollars, state funding for local transportation improvements, assessments on neighboring properties, and revenue from a local option sales tax. The project's goals were to improve safety, increase accessibility and mobility for pedestrians and cyclists, and extend the economic growth from downtown across the bridge.

During the planning process, the city consulted with local stakeholders to create a framework for the project. Area businesses communicated their need for sufficient vehicular access, and residents expressed a desire for pedestrian-oriented spaces. To meet the needs of the area and achieve the project's goals, Rochester formulated a placemaking plan that included upgrading transportation and pedestrian infrastructure, improving the neighborhood's streetscape, and transferring the ownership of the road from the county to the city.

Construction began in 2013 and took two years. In the western section of the corridor, four lanes were reduced to three to address left-turn collisions and to calm speeds. Significant improvements were made along the eastern section by adding bike lanes, landscaped medians, new left-turn lanes within one block of every business, and painted, on-street parking spaces.

To improve the pedestrian environment, each pedestrian crossing in the eastern section was designed to comply with the Americans with Disabilities Act standards. Moreover, crosswalks were painted; sidewalks were widened; two new, lighted intersections and a pedestrian-activated crossing signal were added; pedestrian landings on at least one side of each intersection were installed; and new bus shelters consisting of locally designed artwork were built.

To further enhance the character of the area, new trees, plantings, and benches were incorpo-

rated along the corridor; the neighborhood was renamed "Uptown"; custom art was added to planting protectors; and two light pillars consisting of steel bases, custom tiles, and light-emitting diode lighting were installed at the opposite ends of the district.

Because of these improvements, Uptown is no longer automobile-centric and has become an enticing neighborhood for investment and all forms of transportation. The area's traffic speeds have been reduced from between 45 and 50 miles per hour to 30 miles per hour, which has led to increased pedestrian activity.

Assessed property values in the area grew by 30 percent within the project's first year of completion. Furthermore, blighted properties have gained increased attention from investors. Since the project's completion, Rochester has largely achieved its goals for the corridor: Second Street's safety, economic development, and neighborhood identity have greatly improved.

OPPOSITE: In its previous state (inset), with speeding traffic, limited green space, and few pedestrian amenities, Second Street functioned more as a highway than as a neighborhood street. *(Andrew Masterpole)* Now (top), added medians, bike lanes, ADA-compliant crosswalks, and traffic signals have improved safety. *(Andrew Masterpole)*
TOP: Thanks to the addition of custom-designed bus stops, wayfinding markers, and unique plantings, Uptown is now a distinct neighborhood. *(Andrew Masterpole)*
ABOVE: Custom art, including LED light pillars, helps anchor and enhance the character of the new Uptown District. *(Andrew Masterpole)*

Building a Healthy Corridor

LESSONS FROM DEMONSTRATION CORRIDORS

Demonstration corridors in Denver, Colorado; Boise, Idaho; Los Angeles, California; and Nashville, Tennessee, have been the primary focus of ULI's Healthy Corridors project and have helped shape thinking about what a comprehensively healthy commercial corridor should look and feel like. These activities looked beyond the design of the road and the sidewalks to include bordering neighborhoods, businesses, and communities. ULI district councils have led the work on demonstration corridors at the local level.

ABOVE: Forums at ULI's Spring and Fall Meetings brought together members of the national working group and local leadership groups to discuss health and corridor redevelopment. (Nathan Weber)

A local leadership group was formed for each demonstration corridor and other critical local stakeholders were engaged in workshops that focused on the corridor and on ways the health of the people living, working, and traveling along it could be improved through new partnerships, collaboration, and on-the-ground changes. A primary role of the local leadership group was to ensure that the health needs of the surrounding neighborhoods were considered when redevelopment opportunities were discussed.

In addition, a national working group of 25 experts in land use, development, planning, health, community engagement, and design was formed to guide the project and advise on the work in the demonstration corridors. National working group members engaged with local leadership group members and alumni from the Daniel Rose Fellowship program at two forums in 2015 at ULI's Spring and Fall Meetings. They discussed what health means in the context of commercial corridors, and they planned for local workshops aimed at building partnerships, analyzing corridor conditions, and mapping a path forward.

ABOVE: During the national study visits, experts in a variety of fields toured each corridor, interviewed local stakeholders, and crafted a set of recommendations to help the demonstration corridor create healthier conditions. *(Jess Zimbabwe)*

LEFT: At the local workshops, participants identified the assets and challenges for each corridor. *(Jess Zimbabwe)*

During the summer of 2015, each demonstration corridor held a local workshop to bring together stakeholders and to start or continue a community-wide discussion on how to improve each corridor in ways that promote health. Opportunities, challenges, and key focus areas for each corridor were discussed. Those issues became the basis for national study visits with national working group members and other national experts.

In January and February 2016, the four demonstration corridors held three-day national study visits, when experts in transportation, economic development, health, planning, and design, as well as members of the other demonstration corridors' local leadership groups, provided recommendations to address the key issues impeding each corridor's quest to become a healthier place. The participants toured each corridor, conducted interviews with stakeholders, and ultimately created and presented a set of recommendations to help the demonstration corridor move forward with implementation activities.

Summaries of the activities of each demonstration corridor are presented in the following sections. The summaries include the key issues identified as critical barriers to health-promoting revitalization, as well as recommendations from the national study visits and planned next steps for each corridor.

Federal Boulevard
Denver–Adams County–Westminster, Colorado

Multijurisdictional Area Requires Strong Partnerships

Lessons Learned

» Strong public partnerships are essential when multiple municipalities govern a corridor section.

» Leadership is critical to coordinate multiple governing bodies: one jurisdiction should assume a leadership role in collaboration with the other jurisdiction(s).

ABOVE: Speeding traffic, strip commercial development, and unsafe infrastructure create many challenges for Federal Boulevard. *(James Moore)*

ULI Colorado, in conjunction with many local partners and stakeholders, studied a 2.5-mile segment of Federal Boulevard extending from Regis University in Denver, and passing through unincorporated Adams County, to the city of Westminster. A number of public agencies, private owners, and government entities have jurisdiction or ownership along Federal Boulevard and its adjacent land.

The study segment spans three jurisdictions: the city and county of Denver, Adams County, and Westminster. The three jurisdictions have different standards for streets, zoning, and infrastructure. Separate water districts control the already constrained water infrastructure that future development proposals are required to upgrade. Federal Boulevard itself is a state and federal highway under the jurisdiction of the Colorado Department of Transportation.

The eight-lane corridor is dominated by strip development (including motels, used-car lots, and fast-food restaurants), lacks safe and continuous sidewalks, and is plagued by fast traffic and high rates of pedestrian crashes and injuries. Five low-income census tracts lie adjacent to the corridor and within the study area. A major greenway, Clear Creek, runs under Federal Boulevard, but neighborhood connectivity is limited.

"Federal Boulevard, like many commercial corridors across the country, has economic, social, and built environment conditions that are barriers to improving population health," said Sheila Lynch, local leadership group member and land use program coordinator at the Tri-County Health Department. "The corridor also has many assets, including residents who already call the area home, a university with strong roots, and many community organizations and agencies that are committed to improving community health."

In an effort to better understand these barriers to health as well as the corridor's assets, the Tri-County Health Department completed in 2014 a Health Impact Assessment (HIA) that paralleled an Adams County framework planning process for the majority of the study area. Following an extensive community engagement process and data collection, the HIA provided a set of recommendations to enhance the health perspectives in the framework.

Specifically, the HIA provided 21 recommendations, including recommendations for accommodating safe pedestrian crossings at key

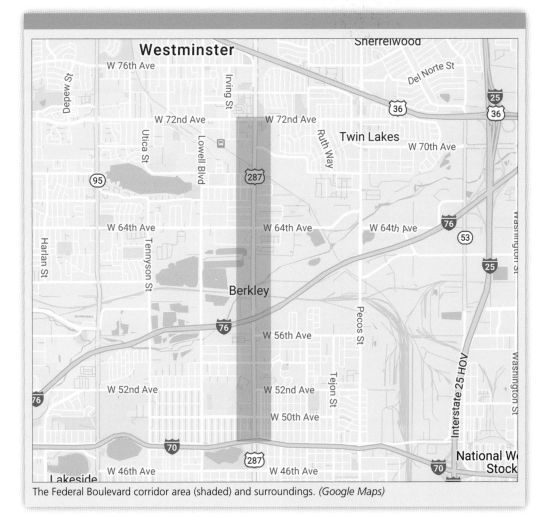

The Federal Boulevard corridor area (shaded) and surroundings. *(Google Maps)*

Quick Facts

» **Length of Study Section:** 2.5 miles

» **Average Number of Lanes:** 6–8 lanes of traffic

» **Average Posted Vehicle Speed:** 35–40 mph

» **Available Transit Options:** Bus

» **Bike Lanes:** 0 miles

» **Sidewalks:** 59 percent of the corridor is missing sidewalks.

» **Income Data:** 53 percent of residents are low-income (defined as below 200 percent of the census-defined poverty level).

» **Corridor Population:** 13,978

» **Ethnicity:** 61.9 percent Hispanic, 23.6 percent other people of color.

» **Land Use:** Dominated by strip land uses such as motels, used-car lots, fast-food restaurants, and poorly maintained mobile home parks.

» **Upcoming Projects:** Regis University campus revitalization; completion of 17.5-acre Aria development; and two transit stations along the corridor: the Gold Line station at 60th and Federal, and the Northwest commuter rail station at 72nd and Federal.

» **Distinguishing Features:** The Clear Creek Greenway is adjacent but currently inaccessible.

intersections along the corridor; having zoning mechanisms that support mixed-use development, neighborhood-serving retail, and healthy food retail; developing strategies for creating and preserving affordable housing along the corridor; and considering an improved identity and brand for the corridor.

Local Work for Change

New and planned developments point to progress along Federal Boulevard. Two new light-rail stations, which opened in 2016, are spurring adjacent mixed-use development. In addition, Aria—a health-focused, mixed-use development located along Federal Boulevard—has partnered with Regis University and the Colorado Health Foundation on Cultivate Health, a program designed to promote healthier living for area residents.

Federal Boulevard's local leadership group, composed of local experts in health, planning, design, development, and community engagement, analyzed the current situation and planning documents. Those documents included the Adams County Framework Plan, the 2014 HIA conducted by the Tri-County Health Depart-

ment, and a number of distinct development plans for property along the corridor. The group determined that the primary challenge was not to create a plan for the corridor but to stitch together various plans into a comprehensive guide that would create a truly healthy corridor that is walkable and bike-friendly; has access to healthy food; and provides economic opportunities and new, high-quality affordable housing. This effort will require substantial interagency and intergovernmental cooperation.

A local stakeholder workshop was held at Regis University in July 2015. About 40 partners representing various viewpoints and organizations attended a day of presentations and small group activities, including a discussion about the importance of leading with health in redevelopment discussions and a mapping exercise to identify the gaps in services and amenities needed to support existing residents along the corridor.

Three groups of participants worked to identify quick wins at three prominent corridor nodes: 52nd and Federal, 60th and Federal, and 72nd and Federal. Opportunities identified included improving health programming for residents, build-

the corridor redevelopment process, and it identified a set of next steps. The workshop successfully achieved buy-in and engagement of diverse stakeholders and the three political jurisdictions that govern the study section. The focus on health helped engage the health and community development sectors.

"While adding health as a guiding principle to this work initially appears to add complexity to an already multifaceted decision-making process, we found that there are real improvements that come to a redevelopment plan that integrates health with other guiding principles, such as traffic analysis, placemaking, economic development, and demographics," said Dave Thorpe, managing director of Silverwest Hotels and chair of the Federal Boulevard local leadership group. "We 'discovered' that when a place helps people live a healthier life, they likely want to stop there, shop there, work there, live there, and raise their family there."

Recommendations

Key issues that arose during the local workshop included the need to improve sidewalks and connectivity, enhance opportunities for new retail and services, and upgrade water infrastructure. Once identified, those issues helped frame the questions for the national study visit, held in January 2016.

STUDY QUESTIONS:

» How can the three jurisdictions work together to promote health?

» What are the opportunities for new retail along the corridor?

» What types of funding and partnership strategies would be best?

» How can concerns about gentrification and displacement be addressed?

» What is the lead role for each stakeholder entity?

ing new sidewalks and bike trails to connect the new transit station and the Clear Creek Greenway, making bus stop improvements, allowing pop-up farmers markets on vacant lots, and encouraging improved partnerships between key organizations that are along and govern Federal Boulevard.

The group also brainstormed strategic positioning statements for the inclusion of health within

Leveraging Anchor Institutions

Anchor institutions, such as Regis University, are important partners in corridor redevelopment projects due to their resources and reach into communities. "Institutions with longstanding presence in their communities, such as universities, contribute to a vital community by virtue of mission, relationships, and resources," said Susan Scherer, associate

dean in the Rueckert-Hartman College for Health Professions at Regis. "Regis University and Urban Ventures have developed a strong partnership based on a shared vision for a healthy community along Federal Boulevard, characterized by access to healthy food and active living."

Urban Ventures, the developer of Aria, partnered with Regis on Cultivate Health, a new program

supported by the Colorado Health Foundation designed to promote healthy living. "We bring different strengths to this partnership," said Scherer. "Regis has students and faculty who can study and implement community-based programs, while Urban Ventures has the expertise in city infrastructure connections and improvements. Working together, the area ad-

jacent to Federal Boulevard now has a community farm, exercise and nutrition programming, and soon will have street improvements to improve walkability. We believe we are all stronger when we work together and include expertise from many different types of community partners."

Participants in the Federal Boulevard national study visit included experts in planning, design, health, market analysis, and economic development.

Key recommendations included the following:

COALESCE DEVELOPMENT AROUND FOUR ACTIVITY NODES located at key intersections: one in Denver, two in Adams County, and one in Westminster. Those nodes should be places to coordinate public investment and concentrate private development, craft unique identities, improve the retail opportunities along the corridor, and enhance the built environment. Two of the nodes (one in Adams County and one in Westminster) are also the locations of new transit stations.

LEVERAGE EXISTING DEVELOPMENT and anchor institutions, including Regis University, to better serve existing residents.

USE NEW INFRASTRUCTURE—such as medians, an enhanced roadway edge, and new connections to existing trails—to connect neighborhoods across the corridor.

REDUCE TRAFFIC SPEEDS to improve safety.

ADDRESS WATER CAPACITY CONSTRAINTS with a comprehensive approach and upfront capital.

IMPLEMENT A DUAL-LEVEL APPROACH TO PARTNERSHIPS whereby elected officials set policy and a technical group focuses on implementation.

Next Steps

Next steps for the Federal Boulevard Healthy Corridors project include working with Adams County on infrastructure funding and working across the three jurisdictions and with key anchor Regis University to foster an intergovernmental collaboration that supports coordinated and complementary corridor-wide improvements, including pedestrian and bike enhancements. The local leadership group is reviewing the potential of the 2.5-mile section of Federal Boulevard to link the downtown Union Station transit hub, the recently completed light-rail corridors, and the U.S. Route 36 multimodal corridor.

The city of Westminster and Adams County have taken a leadership role to form a coalition of the local organizations and agencies involved in Federal Boulevard redevelopment, with ULI and private developers playing a key role. "There is renewed enthusiasm for collaborative solutions to building a healthy Federal Boulevard," said Lynch. The goals of the coalition, called the Westminster Invest Health Initiative, include fostering collaboration between the organizations, getting buy-in and support from jurisdictional leadership, and focusing on transportation and safety improvements along Federal Boulevard.

OPPOSITE: At the Federal Boulevard local workshop, stakeholders identified challenges and quick wins along the corridor. *(Sara Hammerschmidt)*
ABOVE: Areas of the corridor with newer development, such as the section adjacent to Aria, have wider sidewalks that cater to pedestrians. *(Sara Hammerschmidt)*

Vista Avenue
Boise, Idaho

Using Corridor Revitalization and Placemaking to Establish a Gateway

Lessons Learned

» Survey local businesses and residents to understand their needs and get their input on the meaning of a "healthy corridor."

» Set up a process to guide redevelopment, such as a steering committee with dedicated staff that leads visioning, decision making, and implementation work.

ABOVE: The width of Vista Avenue, along with the automobile-oriented strip commercial land uses and the lack of pedestrian- and bike-friendly infrastructure, is typical of many corridors across the country. *(Guy Hand)*

LEFT: Area stakeholders toured Vista Avenue during the local workshop and analyzed various segments of the corridor. *(Guy Hand)*

Vista Avenue, in Boise, Idaho, serves as a gateway to the city and connects the airport and interstate highway to Boise State University and downtown. With automobile-oriented retail, bars, pawnshops, a mix of converted and generally dilapidated housing, and very few pedestrian-oriented facilities, Vista Avenue exemplifies a typical strip commercial street. ULI Idaho and local partners worked on a 1.7-mile segment of the corridor, which spans four miles in total.

This segment of the corridor bifurcates the Vista and Depot Bench neighborhoods. The Vista neighborhood has some of the lowest livability indicators (including income and single-family home values) in

the city, and it includes a mix of single-family and multifamily housing. Because of the function of Vista Avenue as a gateway to the city and the lack of a relationship to the surrounding neighborhoods, there are ample opportunities to improve the uses and infrastructure of the corridor. These improvements will make the corridor more attractive to visitors while simultaneously improving the health and well-being of neighborhood residents.

Local Work for Change

The Vista Avenue local leadership group held its local stakeholder workshop in June 2015. During the walking tour portion of the workshop, participants

The Vista Avenue corridor area (shaded) and surroundings. *(Google Maps)*

Quick Facts

» **Length of Study Section:** 1.7 miles

» **Average Number of Lanes:** 4–6 lanes of traffic

» **Average Posted Vehicle Speed:** 35–40 mph

» **Available Transit Options:** Bus, 30-minute headways, 7:00 a.m. to 7:00 p.m.

» **Bike lanes:** 0 miles

» **Sidewalks:** The corridor has 4-foot sidewalks adjacent to the street with few sidewalk connections on streets off Vista Avenue; it is not a safe, walkable neighborhood.

» **Income Data:** Median household income is $35,551.

» **Safety:** Vista Avenue carries 23,000 cars a day but has only seven pedestrian crosswalks; from 2011 to 2013, there were 249 accidents on the corridor.

» **Land Use:** Single-family housing, single-story strip commercial, car and tire dealers, automobile repair shops, fast-food restaurants, drive-ins, bars, pawnshops, and adult-entertainment venues.

» **Distinguishing Features:** Vista Avenue acts as a gateway to the city of Boise and connects the airport to I-84, Boise State University, and downtown.

broke into groups to observe and analyze different sections of the corridor. Photos taken by participants were shared with the whole group to start a conversation about the current and desired conditions of the corridor and surrounding neighborhoods.

A diverse group of participants attended, including community stakeholders and local and regional agency representatives. Key issues that emerged from the workshop included the need to improve pedestrian access, reduce lane widths and speeds, and work with business owners to get buy-in on improvements and reinvestment.

The local leadership group then identified next steps, which included developing a vision for the corridor with comprehensive engagement and diverse support, as well as looking at quick wins, including cosmetic improvements. The local team investigated leveraging the gateway aspect of Vista Avenue to help create a stronger identity for the surrounding neighborhoods and increasing the engagement of businesses along the corridor. The outcome of an online survey and in-person interviews with business owners indicated interest in an informal business association and greater-than-expected support for improving nonmotorized access to their businesses.

Recommendations

The national study visit was held in February 2016 and presented the participating national experts with several issues to address.

STUDY QUESTIONS:

» How can the Vista corridor's public infrastructure be reconfigured to improve health and enhance the corridor's function as a gateway?

» What are key placemaking strategies that will help foster activity and drive ongoing reinvestment?

» What are successful processes to create and implement a corridor vision plan?

» How can corridor programming and improvements be funded or financed?

» What is the best organizational structure to champion this effort now and over the long haul?

The national experts assessed the assets and challenges of Vista Avenue and the surrounding neighborhood. They then presented the local leadership group and other stakeholders with a set of recommendations centered on emphasizing

code and a district parking strategy or shared parking plan.

ECONOMIC DEVELOPMENT: Use facade grants and low-interest loans to support local businesses. Promote the redevelopment and reuse of existing buildings and develop prototypes to demonstrate the potential reuse of typical lot types along Vista.

CULTURE, SOCIAL CONNECTIVITY, AND HEALTH: Use placemaking, the arts, and culture to develop and cultivate an identity for Vista Avenue and surrounding neighborhoods. To demonstrate the corridor's potential, implement quick wins such as signage, parklets, community gardens, public art in central nodes, and weekend beautification projects involving the community. Build social capital in the neighborhoods by intentionally engaging the different populations that live and work there. Focus on relationship building and neighborhood partnerships, specifically between the Vista and Depot Bench Neighborhood Associations, the city's Energize Our Neighborhoods initiative, and local businesses.

The national experts also recommended a process to begin realizing these recommendations, starting with the local jurisdictions collaborating to establish a Vista Avenue executive steering committee.

First, the steering committee should conduct an objective assessment of the corridor district; in coordination with the city, the Energize Our

the corridor's role as a gateway and creating a healthier and more vibrant district. The national team noted that achieving these goals will require focusing on infrastructure, land use, economic development, culture, social connectivity, and health.

Key recommendations included the following:

INFRASTRUCTURE: Reduce travel lanes from five to three (one travel lane in each direction, a center turn lane, and protected bike lanes). Expand pedestrian and planting spaces on each side of the street to 12 feet. Support bike connectivity along Vista or parallel streets, add and enhance signals at intersections, and enhance bus stops by including shelters and benches with schedule displays.

LAND USE: Create a mixed-use zoning designation along Vista and implement a form-based

Neighborhoods initiative, the Depot Bench Neighborhood Association, the Ada County Highway District, and other stakeholders, the committee should also develop a unified vision that helps prioritize investments. Second, the steering committee should ensure appropriate staffing by hiring an individual with responsibility for activities related to Vista Avenue and the surrounding neighborhoods. Finally, the committee should evaluate potential funding sources (federal, state, regional, local, and philanthropic) and establish an implementation program and timeline.

Next Steps

Using the recommendations from the national study visit—but recognizing that local elected officials considered some recommendations controversial—the local team identified some next steps in the corridor redevelopment process. The local leadership group first communicated the outcomes of the study visit with the Vista and Depot Bench Neighborhood Associations and with elected officials through presentations and summary documents.

The key to next steps for Vista Avenue redevelopment for local stakeholders is to work closely with the city of Boise. The local leadership group will support city efforts to develop a work plan that implements the study visit recommendations, including suggestions about needed funding and organizational structure. The local team also intends to develop a facilitated visioning process for the corridor that engages residents, local businesses, public agencies, and other key stakeholders.

A potential source of funding under exploration is the tax increment financing that is available through the Capital City Development Corporation. This funding source can be tapped by designating Vista Avenue as an urban redevelopment district. If the redevelopment agency is supportive, the agency staff would work with the city of Boise to develop a master plan and implementation strategies for the district; it would also work with the city of Boise to set priorities for reinvestment in public infrastructure.

In addition, building on the work of the Healthy Corridors project and other local efforts, including ULI Idaho's Moving People First Summit and the city of Boise's Transportation Action Plan, the local team and city partners plan to work with the Ada County Highway District to revise policies for public roadways in ways that will foster health and economic development along the corridor.

The research accomplished and the partnerships established over the two years of the Healthy Corridors project have set the stage for positive changes to occur along Vista Avenue. Bob Taunton, chair of the local leadership group and president of Taunton Group LLC, noted that the lasting value of the Vista corridor demonstration project became clear when community members realized that the corridor, now primarily a throughway for vehicles, could become a community place with a unique identity. "The power of that understanding is driving business owners, residents, and local government to imagine a shared vision for Vista Avenue that will lead to future positive individual and economic health outcomes," Taunton said.

OPPOSITE: One asset of the corridor is the variety of housing types that exist along and adjacent to Vista Avenue. *(Jess Zimbabwe)*
BELOW: Plans for Vista Avenue include developing a master plan and reinvesting in public infrastructure along the corridor. *(Jess Zimbabwe)*

Van Nuys Boulevard
Los Angeles, California

Leveraging Existing Assets to Engage the Community

Lessons Learned

» Capitalize on assets and existing identity, and leverage those assets to draw visitors to the corridor.

» Demonstrate changes to the corridor, whenever possible, through temporary infrastructure improvements and pop-up events; then gauge community response and achieve buy-in from residents and business owners before more permanent improvements are made.

Van Nuys Boulevard in Los Angeles spans the central San Fernando Valley, running about ten miles through communities of varying demographics. ULI Los Angeles and a group of local stakeholders chose to focus on the 0.75-mile stretch of Van Nuys that runs through the heart of the Pacoima neighborhood. Located 30 minutes north of downtown Los Angeles, Pacoima is a vibrant and diverse community that also has some of the city's highest poverty and crime rates and poorest health outcomes. The neighborhood exhibits some of the city's highest concentrations of childhood obesity, diabetes mortality, and stroke. Pacoima is a high-needs neighborhood, with an average per capita yearly income of $13,180 (one of the lowest in the city) and an average median household income well below that of the city. More than one in five Pacoima residents falls

under the federal poverty limit, and one in ten working-age adults in Pacoima are unemployed.

The corridor is characterized by a wide automobile-oriented road, small-scale commercial establishments, inadequate pedestrian and bicycle infrastructure, and adjacent single-family homes. The corridor also contains unique cultural elements, including colorful murals and small businesses that cater to the surrounding Latino community. Melani Smith, a Los Angeles–based urban planner and chair of the local leadership group, described it this way: "Van Nuys is an underperforming area in Los Angeles that at the same time has enormous potential in the power of its engaged community, lively arts scene, and local entrepreneurial spirit."

Van Nuys Boulevard's unique cultural resources and active local organizations provide a strong

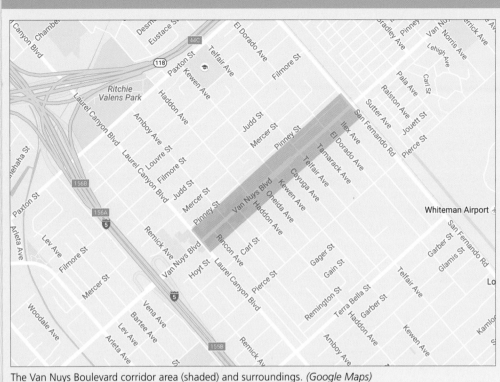

The Van Nuys Boulevard corridor area (shaded) and surroundings. *(Google Maps)*

OPPOSITE: Unique elements, including colorful murals, contribute to the cultural character of the corridor. *(Rosa Ruvalcaba/flickr)*

foundation for enhancing the economic, environmental, and physical health of the community. The street has been identified as one of the 15 "Great Streets" segments being championed throughout the city of Los Angeles by Mayor Eric Garcetti's office, and it is being considered for the route of a new Metro bus rapid transit (BRT) or light-rail line, which would enhance connectivity between the neighborhood and the surrounding area. In addition, a new neighborhood "City Hall" and entrepreneur center have laid the foundation for a transformation rooted in community needs and desires.

Local Work for Change

In the summer of 2015, Van Nuys Boulevard's local leadership group held a stakeholder workshop that brought together the arts, health, business, social service, education, public sector employees, and community stakeholders who had not been connected previously. Participants presented information about the numerous planning efforts for the area, and the group was able to establish a foundation of common understanding around the need to improve the health of those who rely on Van Nuys Boulevard. "Bringing ULIs 'healthy places' and 'healthy corridor' lenses to a place like this led us to bring a range of stakeholders to the table that had not collaborated together previously," Smith noted.

During the workshop, the local leadership group presented summaries of past plans for the area and tied them together as an overall wish list for the neighborhood. Items on the list included pedestrian- and bike-friendly amenities and residents' desires to turn Van Nuys into a quieter, cleaner, and safer corridor. In an interactive discussion, the stakeholders considered how a healthy corridor is defined, what elements currently exist, and what elements are needed along Van Nuys. The group also discussed ideas for a pilot project along Van Nuys that would demonstrate its potential as a healthy corridor, and the group considered who should be involved in that project.

Key issues that emerged during the workshop included the need to improve the perception and reality of safety (including traffic, crime, and gang activity), encourage education and training tied to the arts and culture scene, find new uses to improve economic and public health, and engage all populations and ages in decisions that affect the corridor.

Another big challenge in this area is housing; numerous single-family houses have been illegally converted into multifamily dwellings, thus creating extremely dense and potentially dangerous living conditions. The Los Angeles City Council District office intends to maintain the affordability of the area while converting the illegal conversions into formalized—and safe—residential options that meet building codes.

Recommendations

The local workshop helped bring area stakeholders together to discuss current and potential issues concerning Van Nuys Boulevard. It also set the stage and identified study questions for the national study visit held in February 2016.

STUDY QUESTIONS:

» In an economically and environmentally challenged but culturally rich area such as Pacoima, what opportunities exist for improving the health and economic well-being of the community, whether through providing jobs, services, or goods?

» How can Van Nuys Boulevard property owners take advantage of the imminent opportunity presented by a proposed new transit line and other investments in the corridor to develop businesses now and prevent displacement in the future?

The national experts reviewed the assets and challenges of Van Nuys Boulevard. Assets include a high percentage of homeownership in the area, an entrepreneurial spirit, and a corridor that has continuous sidewalks with buildings adjacent to the road rather than set back from it. Conversely, a clearly automobile-dominated street with high traffic speeds and few pedestrian and bike amenities creates a challenging environment. A lack of business diversity, as well as a lack of businesses that remain open after 5:00 p.m., creates challenges to serving daily community needs. In addition, a lack of policies or regulations to support the creation of safe accessory dwelling units has contributed to the current housing concerns.

To emphasize the existing assets, the participants created a three-pronged value structure for a healthy Van Nuys Boulevard that highlights the strong arts and culture in the community, the opportunity for change, and the diversity of the area. The team provided recommendations in three overarching categories: community health and development, economic development, and marketing strategies focused on getting people to the boulevard. Those categories framed specific recommendations, including ideas for introducing programming, expanding opportunities for local businesses through training and an organizational structure, and embracing social media and the arts to bring people to the corridor.

Key recommendations included the following:

PLACEMAKING AND PROGRAMMING: Leverage social connectedness through strategies including enhancing active transportation safety, convenience, and aesthetics; producing regular marquee events and programming, such as a chalk-art street mural festival that celebrates Pacoima's unique and diverse culture; cultivating a "Pacoima Week" that celebrates local culture, community, and food; participating in CicLAvia or other Great Streets events that are supported by the mayor's office and that occur along Van Nuys; and creating places for the community to gather outdoors.

PUBLIC SAFETY: Improve the perception of safety in the area by facilitating agreements among businesses to stay open later; by promoting family-friendly and active spaces, businesses, and activities; and by working with the local library to become even further involved with the community.

HOUSING: Encourage healthy housing in Pacoima by allowing and streamlining the permitting process for multiple-family units.

HEALTHY FOOD: Increase access to healthy food by creating a location on the corridor where residents can sell neighborhood produce on a regular

basis; by identifying an existing restaurant in the San Fernando Valley and developing tools to encourage it to locate in Pacoima; and by enhancing education around food growing, production, and safety.

LOCAL BUSINESSES: Build up the entrepreneurial ecosystem of Van Nuys by expanding business development opportunities, promoting and featuring local businesses, and providing training and mentorship opportunities to local business owners.

MARKETING AND IDENTITY: Leverage opportunities, including a logo for the "Celebrate Pacoima" tagline; embrace hashtags like #celebratepacoima and #muralmile; invest in street-lamp banners to highlight the corridor; and look at new events including a "Pacoima at Night" night market and evening art walks. Define a "heart of Pacoima" through street and infrastructure transformation and a murals program that highlights the history of Pacoima.

The national study group participants recommended that the local team and stakeholders prioritize the following: demonstrate street infrastructure transformation on one section of Van Nuys Boulevard, use city resources to create a city liaison position to work with local businesses, and position Pacoima City Hall as a catalyst for change by using the space for programs and events.

Next Steps

At the inception of the Healthy Corridors project in early 2015, the ULI Los Angeles staff and members started working with Los Angeles Mayor Eric Garcetti's office, 7th District councilmember Felipe Fuentes and his staff, and local stakeholders to envision how Van Nuys Boulevard could be improved in health-promoting ways.

Through research and conversations with local organizations and public officials, the team recognized very early in the project that for many years the community and consultant teams had offered many great ideas for making Pacoima a healthier place to live. Those ideas ranged from encouraging physical activity and creating safer environments to improving access to healthy food. With such ideas in mind, the local leadership group planned a demonstration project that would allow community members to see, feel, and experience what a healthier Van Nuys Boulevard could be.

On March 6, 2016, Van Nuys Boulevard was closed to automobiles as part of CicLAvia, a recurring open-streets event that catalyzes good health, active transportation, and lively public spaces. ULI Los Angeles worked with partners and stakeholders in Pacoima to plan the Pacoima Health Zone—a demonstration project modeling

the potential long-term changes that would result from creating a more vibrant, healthy, and people-friendly Van Nuys Boulevard.

ULI Los Angeles and members constructed pop-up streetscape elements, including a temporary parklet and curb extensions. Other area partners provided information, demonstrations, and interactive exercises intended to create healthier people and places. The purpose of the Health Zone was not only to show what a healthy corridor—and a healthy Pacoima—could look like but also to help build a constituency for and relationships to support greater access to health resources.

Along this section of Van Nuys, a lane reduction to be completed by the end of 2016 will improve the safety and walkability of the corridor. The local leadership group is working on enhancing the arts and culture focus of the corridor, and the group continues to work with community partners to support the partners' work in Pacoima. The group is also developing a plan to implement national study visit recommendations, including the recommendation to continue community programs and local business enhancement and retention and the recommendation to identify funding sources.

Through those efforts, progress is underway to transform Van Nuys Boulevard into a healthier, more complete street.

OPPOSITE TOP: During the national study visit, experts toured Van Nuys Boulevard and the surrounding neighborhoods. *(Sara Hammerschmidt)*
OPPOSITE BOTTOM: A wide, automobile-oriented road prevents safe walking and biking along and across Van Nuys Boulevard. *(Jonathan Nettler)*
TOP: The Pacoima Health Zone included information booths, pop-up infrastructure projects, healthy living demonstrations, and interactive exercises. *(ULI Los Angeles)*
ABOVE: A temporary parklet constructed during CicLAvia served to illustrate what more permanent street improvements could look like. *(ULI Los Angeles)*

Charlotte Avenue
Nashville, Tennessee

Developing a Strategy for Ownership and Connectivity to Improve Health Along the Corridor

Lessons Learned
» Identify quick wins demonstrating improvements to placemaking, health, and streetscape that can be easily implemented at key nodes or locations along the corridor.

» Establish a corridor oversight group to champion and lead the implementation of improvements.

ABOVE AND INSET: Uncoordinated development, unsightly utility poles, and nonexistent safe pedestrian infrastructure are some of the challenges facing Charlotte Avenue. *(Jess Zimbabwe)*

Charlotte Avenue is a main traffic throughway from downtown Nashville to the western suburbs. ULI Nashville and partners worked on a four-mile segment of Charlotte Avenue near downtown.

The neighborhoods north of Charlotte Avenue between I-40 and I-440 are historically home to a majority African American population and cultural arts centers and universities, including Fisk University and Meharry Medical College. These neighborhoods face greater health-related social and economic challenges than the rest of Nashville faces.

The area is 81.5 percent African American compared with 27.7 percent for Nashville as a whole.

The area's poverty rate at 44.8 percent is more than double that of Nashville. Only 6.2 percent of residents have a bachelor's degree or higher, which is less than half the rate for residents of Nashville overall. This area also experiences worse health outcomes than Nashville as a whole: in 2013, the hospitalization rates for both hypertension and diabetes were roughly three times higher than the rates for the city overall.

Alongside and just south of Charlotte Avenue is Nashville's unofficial and longstanding Medical District, which includes the Metro Public Health Department and HCA Corporate offices, as well as institutions such as the Centennial Medical Center, the American Cancer Society, and the Red Cross.

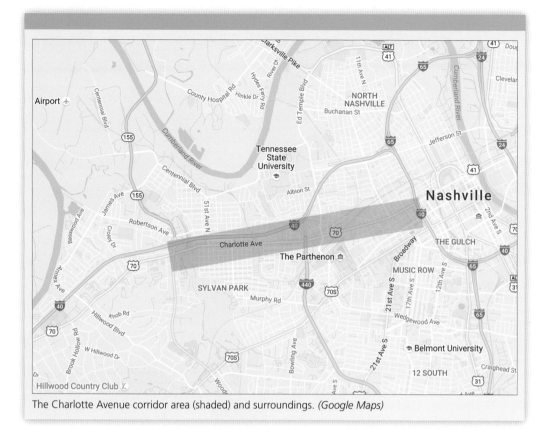

The Charlotte Avenue corridor area (shaded) and surroundings. *(Google Maps)*

Quick Facts

» **Length of Study Section:** 3.9 miles

» **Average Number of Lanes:** 4–5 lanes of traffic

» **Average Posted Vehicle Speed:** 40 mph

» **Available Transit Options:** Bus rapid transit (BRT) lite

» **Bike Lanes:** Unprotected bike lanes run along the majority of the corridor in both directions, with sharrows in some smaller areas; there are no bike lanes or sharrows on the western one-fourth of the corridor.

» **Sidewalks:** The corridor has sidewalks on both sides of the street except at the western end of the corridor.

» **Income Data:** The corridor has a mix of income levels: south of the corridor is higher income; north of the corridor is lower income.

» **Land Use:** On the southern side is Nashville's longstanding Medical District with large anchor hospitals, but there is an opportunity for continued civic and streetscape improvements and commercial and multifamily infill. On the northern side are Nashville's historically African American neighborhoods, cultural arts centers, and universities. The western section of the corridor has more typically automobile-oriented uses such as strip malls, repair shops, and fast-food restaurants.

Currently, there is a great deal of interest in and plans for both public and private investment and development along Charlotte Avenue. But development patterns appear uncoordinated, and uses and infrastructure are not adequate to support the needs of adjacent neighborhood residents.

Local Work for Change

The Nashville local leadership group saw an immediate opportunity to implement more strategic principles, actions, and partnerships that support and improve the health of the adjacent neighborhoods and business users. The Metropolitan Government of Nashville and Davidson County (Metro Nashville) and its mayor, Megan Barry, who was elected in the fall of 2015, identified eight corridors across the city on which to focus redevelopment efforts, including Charlotte Avenue. Short- and long-term implementation strategies that focus on creating a healthier Charlotte Avenue may be replicated along the other corridors as well.

New development is occurring along Charlotte. A new 19-acre community called oneC1TY focuses on principles of healthy living and sustainable design and, when completed, will include a mix of office, residential, retail, hotel, and open space.

Recently finished complete streets projects near the corridor—the 28th/31st Avenue Connector and the 11th Avenue Complete Street Project, which both intersect with Charlotte Avenue—provide local examples of what a redeveloped road could look like. However, the goal of the local leadership group was to look beyond the travel lanes of the corridor and address the health and connectivity problems residents of adjacent neighborhoods experience.

"We selected the Charlotte Avenue corridor due to the demographic and land use diversity it offered within the neighborhoods it connects," said Ryan Doyle, general manager at OneC1TY Nashville and chair of the local leadership group. "While this made for a broad set of opinions through our community meetings, it has been inspiring to see cohesiveness begin to build about the importance of a more holistic approach to developing the area and giving the citizens an opportunity to improve their health."

The Charlotte Avenue local workshop, held in August 2015 with about 100 local stakeholders, identified health assets and barriers along the corridor. Small groups looked at maps and images of one-mile segments of the corridor to identify where basic services or amenities were missing, what components of new development projects should be included to positively affect the health of residents and workers in the area, what incentives and funding are available to ensure that those components are included, and what investments should be prioritized by the city government.

Drawing on input from the local workshop, the local leadership group cultivated a set of implementable quick wins, both in the short and long term. The team is considering a number of strategies, including urban agriculture, active play spaces, programs designed to empower at-risk youth, and rebranding and education efforts developed in conjunction with local partners.

During the fall of 2015, the local leadership group partnered with Vanderbilt University to conduct interviews and surveys with residents as part of an action research class. The class engaged with the local communities along Charlotte Avenue to understand the effects of past development projects on residents, the problems with access to healthy food along the corridor, and the experiences of residents who rely on the corridor for daily activities.

Recommendations

During the local workshop, the local leadership group identified four priority areas on which to focus short- and long-term action-oriented projects:

1. PROJECTS THAT IMPROVE HEALTH, placemaking, and connectivity;

2. AN IMPROVEMENT DISTRICT to guide development along the corridor;

3. APPROPRIATE FUNDING SOURCES; and

4. A POSSIBLE DEVELOPMENT OVERLAY for Charlotte Avenue.

Those priority areas guided a set of questions that the group prepared for the national study visit with national experts in January 2016.

STUDY QUESTIONS:

» How do we promote health along the corridor?

» How do we bring together champions for change and keep people engaged over the long haul?

» How can or should corridor improvements be funded and financed?

» What are quick wins or opportunities for immediate action?

The national study visit participants included experts on placemaking, transportation, real estate development, business improvement districts, planning, design, and economic development. They presented observations about and recommendations for Charlotte Avenue to a group of local stakeholders at a public meeting. Discussion touched on understanding the urgent need to develop a comprehensive health strategy that would counteract development pressures and obsolete infrastructure, as well as on the need to address corridor challenges prior to, or concurrent with, new development opportunities that would make health-focused redevelopment easier to implement.

Identified assets that are unique to the corridor included a number of cultural resources, adjacent greenways, BRT lite, passionate stakeholders, and unique neighborhoods and pockets of vibrancy. Identified challenges included automobile-oriented infrastructure, limited fresh food options, sidewalks with unfavorable pedestrian conditions, and neighborhoods that are isolated because of the location of roads and freeways.

Key recommendations included the following:

ORGANIZATIONAL STRATEGIES: Identify champions to create an entity ("Friends of Charlotte Avenue") with a full-time leader to help implement priority initiatives along the corridor. Engage and coordinate residents and businesses, and aim to create a business improvement district or corridor improvement district in the future. Encourage the Richland Park area of Charlotte Avenue to become a "village" or node along the corridor.

CORRIDOR CONNECTIVITY: Implement low-cost, small-scale approaches as a first step to improve safety and infrastructure along the corridor (such as painted crosswalks and public art projects). Prioritize infrastructure changes such as widening sidewalks along Charlotte Avenue, adding a buffer between traffic lanes and pedestrians, adding pedestrian crossings and pedestrian-activated signals, enhancing lighting, minimizing curb cuts, activating the street level in new developments, and encouraging or requiring developers to build an improved public realm on their property. Leverage existing BRT with signal prioritization, improved pedestrian access, real-time arrival information, and (in the long term) dedicated lanes.

FOOD ACCESS: Focus new healthy food options on the neighborhoods north of Charlotte that have the poorest health outcomes. Consider implementing new, healthy, fast-casual or daytime food businesses near medical buildings and hospitals. Identify public funding sources to help support the development of full-service grocery stores along the corridor, which can also create jobs for local residents.

FUNDING: Look to private sector seed investment to establish the corridor's organizing entity. Leverage tax increment financing, and use Charlotte as a corridor demonstration project for building and infrastructure improvements. Identify major employers, foundations, and other anchor institutions that will fund specific pieces

of the Charlotte Avenue redevelopment effort. Those institutions can also contribute to the local economy by subsidizing mortgage loans for their staff members to live in properties near Charlotte. For example, the University of Pennsylvania offers employees a $7,500 loan, forgivable after five years of employment, to assist them in purchasing homes near campus.

Next Steps

Based on recommendations from the national experts, the local leadership group is identifying nodes along the Charlotte Avenue corridor to serve as sites for piloting improvements and demonstrating what a healthy corridor could look like. The group is working in collaboration with the mayor's office and the Metropolitan Development and Housing Association to create a corridor coalition, an organization that will continue to manage healthy corridor strategies not only along Charlotte Avenue but also throughout the city of Nashville.

"Improving the health of the Charlotte Avenue corridor is about building connections. It's about creating places that connect to the surrounding neighborhoods, about building connections between diverse stakeholders, and connecting new developments to Nashville's parks and greenways," said John Vick, an epidemiologist with the Metro Nashville Public Health Department and member of the local leadership group. "We hope that as Charlotte Avenue transforms, it serves as an example of how to build places where health is a natural part of the decision-making and design process, where healthy choices become the easiest choices and are accessible to everyone."

INSET: National experts recommended that local stakeholders focus their efforts on starting a corridor-focused organization, identifying funding sources, and examining issues of connectivity and access to healthy food. *(ULI Nashville)*

BELOW: Encouraging an improved public realm, such as mural projects on blank walls, can enhance the pedestrian environment along Charlotte. *(Jess Zimbabwe)*

4 Getting from Here to There

PLANNING AND IMPLEMENTING IMPROVEMENTS

Creating a healthy corridor will require a clear vision and robust partnerships. This section presents ten key principles for healthy corridor development, along with a process for creating a healthier corridor. The principles were developed through the two-year engagement with the demonstration corridor teams in Denver, Boise, Los Angeles, and Nashville. The principles are broadly applicable to commercial corridors across the country that are striving to become healthy, equitable, sustainable, and vibrant places. Moreover, the principles should be shared with stakeholders and community members at the start of a healthy corridor planning process.

Although it will take strong partnerships with many stakeholders to initiate an effort to create a healthier corridor, it is likely that one primary organization will start the conversations. This primary organization may be a public sector organization (such as a planning, health, or transportation department); a group of concerned residents or community advocates; or a group of private sector developers or business owners. Whoever initiates the conversation must strategically and thoughtfully reach out to the other stakeholders and must determine which groups can undertake each of the principles and responsibilities when crafting and scoping an action plan to build a healthier corridor.

Ten Principles for Healthy Corridor Development

1 USE THE LENS OF HEALTH TO CONVENE LOCAL STAKEHOLDERS, especially stakeholders who may be considered "unusual suspects," including public health professionals and hospitals. Leverage anchor institutions (including hospitals, major employers, and universities) as key financial and research partners, especially if they are located near the corridor. Anchors are typically economic generators with civic power, and corridor champions can engage each institution to help identify what types of investments it could make in the corridor.

2 IDENTIFY CHAMPIONS. Redeveloping the corridor in a holistically healthy way will require leadership and alignment from many partners, but identifying a small number of champions—from local government and the community—to lead and further progress can help ensure that on-the-ground changes become a reality.

3 UNDERSTAND THE CONTEXT OF THE CORRIDOR, AND DETERMINE HOW JURISDICTIONAL BOUNDARIES AFFECT THE CORRIDOR. If the corridor is within one jurisdiction, building consensus and making changes will likely be easier to achieve. If the corridor spans more than one jurisdiction, forming partnerships between municipal agencies will be necessary to reach consensus on a vision, a process, and implementation strategies for the entire corridor. Using the health lens and the overarching vision of a healthy corridor may also be a powerful way to draw in and engage stakeholders from various jurisdictions.

4 ANALYZE AND UNDERSTAND THE CORRIDOR'S DEVELOPMENT POTENTIAL. Is the corridor in a hot market where new development is rapidly taking place, an emerging market just beginning to attract developers, or a potential market where no new development is occurring? By understanding the current market and community needs, stakeholders and project leaders can determine the urgency of implementation, select intervention strategies designed to promote health, and identify and rethink land uses and zoning that are incompatible with community needs.

5 CREATE A LONG-TERM CORRIDOR VISION STRATEGY WHILE ALSO DELIVERING QUICK WINS. All stakeholders should be engaged in a visioning process to determine the future look and feel of the corridor based on the context and community needs. Demonstrating quick wins and progress—through projects such as pop-up farmers markets or temporary lane reductions—can help the community understand and appreciate future changes.

6 PROACTIVELY IDENTIFY AND ADDRESS TRANSPORTATION AND INFRASTRUCTURE CHALLENGES. Work to pair improvements—such as sidewalk and bike lane installation, safe pedestrian crossings, and utility undergrounding—with road and infrastructure projects already planned by the city or jurisdiction.

7 ENGAGE PROACTIVELY WITH COMMUNITIES AND ADVOCACY GROUPS ALONG THE CORRIDOR, and create and support municipal strategies to encourage continued diversity and mitigate displacement. These strategies include inclusionary zoning, public housing subsidies, and ownership interest provided to tenants.

8 ENGAGE WITH BUSINESS OWNERS AND LANDOWNERS. Local businesses that serve the corridor should be allowed and encouraged to remain and thrive. Setting up a BID or an association of local businesses can help existing businesses identify needs for future changes as well as funding sources for their own improvements. A BID or a similar organization would keep business owners updated on progress.

9 FACILITATE HEALTHY FOOD ACCESS THROUGH RETAIL AND POLICY SOLUTIONS. The healthy food movement—from community gardens to farmers markets to farm-to-table restaurants—is gaining traction within the real estate industry, according to *Emerging Trends in Real Estate® 2016*. The growing interest in urban agriculture could be leveraged to attract new food business to the corridor. A careful analysis of the needs of the surrounding community—in terms of what is currently available and affordable—should guide outreach to new vendors and developers.

10 THERE IS NO ONE SOURCE OF FUNDING: SEEK OUT MULTIPLE OPPORTUNITIES FROM PUBLIC AND PRIVATE SOURCES. The assortment of applicable funding strategies will likely depend on the context of the corridor. For a menu of funding opportunities, download the "Building Healthy Corridors: Strategy and Resource Guide" from uli.org/healthycorridors.

OPPOSITE: Low-cost quick wins and demonstration projects can include temporary streetscape improvements, festivals, and community art projects. *(ULI Los Angeles)*

ABOVE: When convening local stakeholders, use the lens of health to identify new partners. *(Guy Hand)*

A Process for Change

Relying on strong partnerships as well as stakeholder and community engagement, the recommended process draws from the experiences of champions—which include developers, community advocates, residents, and the public sector—who are pushing for change in corridors across the country.

The following process roadmap for creating a healthy corridor outlines a "gold standard" approach for ensuring that the community and its needs, specifically those relating to health, are at the forefront of corridor redevelopment processes and that plans are carried out to fruition.

Phase I—Startup and Partnership Development (Six to Nine Months)

The first phase, spanning six to nine months, is focused on starting the project, developing partnerships, and identifying stakeholders and resources to support corridor redevelopment activities. Typically, this first step in the process of transforming a corridor would be led by the city or municipality. It is critical to identify a multisectoral leadership group of eight to ten members who meet regularly to guide the project, but it is also critical to identify a larger group of local stakeholders.

Another important initial step is to conduct an audit of the corridor (using the Healthy Corridor Audit Tool, which can be downloaded at uli.org/healthycorridors) to understand the baseline physical and social conditions of the corridor and the surrounding neighborhoods.

Initial meetings with stakeholders and the community should occur during Phase I. In these initial meetings, private and public sector stakeholders should focus on coalition building and defining and setting an overall framework for creating a healthy corridor. Community members and advocates should focus on discussing a specific vision for a healthier corridor, what people like and dislike about the current corridor conditions, and the community's needs.

The leadership group should ensure that the meetings are integrated into existing community meetings, such as those held by neighborhood associations, church groups, community event planners, and local businesses. The meetings should solicit as much resident and business owner input and engagement as possible. Drawing on those meetings, the leadership group should work on a draft vision statement for the healthier future of the corridor.

Phase II—Convenings and Issue Identification (Three to Four Months)

Phase II focuses on convenings and issue identification, which will be based on the preliminary meetings that occurred in Phase I. The leadership group should convene a public workshop with the local stakeholders and community members to review the draft vision statement and audit results, identify corridor assets and challenges, and start setting priorities for needed changes.

The public workshop should adopt the following goals:

» Align local stakeholders and community members (including state and local agencies, community group leaders, social and environmental advocacy groups, residents, representatives from any anchor institutions, and public health professionals).

» Assess the current state of planning, investment, and metrics and the current focus on health.

» Identify gaps and obstacles to change.

» Identify opportunities for quick wins.

» Identify needed resources and expertise.

An optional activity during this phase is to convene a two- to three-day study visit of national experts who should be selected according to the needs identified at the public workshop. The goal of this study visit is to focus on key issues and challenges that have been identified during the public workshop.

Six to seven targeted national experts would work with the leadership group to take healthy corridor efforts to the next level and provide strategic advice about key issues, recommendations, and action priorities. Suggestions would come from an objective outsider viewpoint to help re-envision the corridor as a holistically healthy place.

Sample agendas for the local and national convenings can be found at uli.org/healthycorridors.

OPPOSITE: Proactively identify and address transportation and infrastructure challenges to create a healthier corridor. *(Sara Hammerschmidt)*
ABOVE: Stakeholder meetings should focus on coalition building and determining a vision for a healthy corridor. *(Jess Zimbabwe)*
BELOW: Local workshops should engage stakeholders in identifying corridor assets and existing challenges to healthy corridor redevelopment. *(Guy Hand)*

Phase III—Priority Setting and Quick Wins (Three to Four Months)

Phase III includes setting priorities for achieving the healthy corridor vision and for implementing recommendations and solutions for the identified challenges. Drawing on the local workshop and the optional study visit with national experts, the leadership group should set priorities for implementation, including quick wins and short-, medium-, and long-term actions.

In addition, the group should outline policy changes needed to achieve the priorities; these changes might include rezoning, establishing a tax increment financing district, and amending housing policies. This phase also includes determining appropriate funding sources and needed partnerships; beginning work to secure funding, which includes targeting federal, state, and local funds, foundations, and philanthropy; and partnering with anchor institutions along the corridor or in the area.

Additional actions during this phase include the implementation of low-cost quick wins, demonstration projects, or tactical urbanism projects such as temporary lane reductions, curb extensions, and pop-up public plazas. Such changes will show the community what healthy changes along the corridor could look like. The leadership group should also work with all stakeholders to develop design and land use strategies to improve connectivity, safety, road conditions, and buildings.

Phase IV—Implementation and Working for Change (Nine to 12 Months)

Phase IV is focused on executing the plans developed and the priorities set in earlier phases. More permanent development, policy, planning, and programming changes (such as road reconfiguration, tree planting, sidewalk widening, other infrastructure changes, and festivals and farmers markets) should be implemented during this phase.

Phase IV is also when a corridor oversight group should be assembled as a first step in ensuring that implementation plans progress. This group should include a paid staff person who has primary responsibility for coordination and implementation moving forward. This position could be a part-time assignment for an existing municipal employee, or it could be a new position housed within an existing city office or in a nonprofit created to oversee corridor revitalization.

Phase V—Sustaining Progress and Avoiding Problems

The final phase focuses on sustaining progress and avoiding problems after implementation. A plan for ongoing corridor maintenance and redevelopment should be created, and—if desired—a BID or corridor improvement district should be implemented to maintain and further the creation of a healthy corridor (see "Building Healthy Corridors: Strategy and Resource Guide" at uli.org/healthycorridors for more information).

In an effort to avoid unforeseen issues, changes should be measured and tracked. One of the best approaches would be to conduct another audit using the Healthy Corridor Audit Tool and then continue to repeat the audit periodically—after on-the-ground changes have been initiated—to track progress.

Healthy Corridor Roadmap

PHASE I: Startup and Partnership Development (six to nine months)	» Identify a diverse leadership and stakeholder group » Pursue strategies for community empowerment, engagement, and coalition building, framed around health and community needs » Conduct initial-conditions audit
PHASE II: Convenings and Issue Identification (three to four months)	» Hold a local public workshop to identify key corridor assets and challenges » Start setting priorities for needed changes » Hold study visits to obtain expert recommendations
PHASE III: Priority Setting and Quick Wins (three to four months)	» With stakeholders, set priorities with quick wins and short-, medium-, and long-term actions » Outline policy changes needed to achieve priorities » Determine appropriate funding sources and needed partnerships » Implement low-cost quick wins
PHASE IV: Implementation and Working for Change (nine to 12 months)	» Execute on plans and priorities developed in previous phases » Implement longer-term development, policy, planning, and programming interventions » Assemble a corridor oversight group to oversee implementation
PHASE V: Sustaining Progress and Avoiding Problems (ongoing)	» Sustain progress through the creation of a formal leadership group or improvement district » Measure and track changes, and conduct conditions audits periodically » Plan for ongoing maintenance and redevelopment » Continue to address affordability and displacement issues

ABOVE: A holistically healthy corridor is created from design, land use patterns, infrastructure, and programming that support the people who live, work, and travel along it. *(Craig Kuhner)*

In addition, the ongoing maintenance and redevelopment plan should include ways to track corridor affordability so that residents and local business owners can gauge the potential of displacement. The plan should also describe ways to create contingency plans and to prepare for needed policy changes that will allow current residents and business owners to stay in the neighborhood once the corridor has been improved.

Building a Healthier Corridor

Using a lens of health during corridor revitalization projects has many benefits. Social engagement, the physical health of residents, the economic health of local businesses, and public safety can all be improved when taking a holistic approach to corridor redevelopment that looks at the needs of those who live, work, and travel along commercial corridors.

When the design and land use patterns that support community needs are considered, positive transformations can be anticipated. In fact, strategies that engage and support those who live along or use a corridor on a regular basis help ensure that commercial corridors are transformed from automobile-dominated and outdated retail strips to safe, healthy, vibrant, mixed-use places with next-generation infrastructure and linkages to other parts of the city.

Using healthy corridor principles to guide the work, the process roadmap for change should be a collaborative effort involving all types of stakeholders, including residents, advocacy groups, businesses, public agencies, and private developers. To create healthier corridors that will benefit all who live, work, and travel along them, it is critical to work in partnerships. It is also critical to engage residents—who tend to be lower-income people and families that do not typically have a voice in community decision-making processes—to understand their needs and concerns.

By creating strong partnerships and using a strategy that focuses on developing such partnerships, identifying key issues, setting priorities, implementing changes, and monitoring progress, corridors across the United States can be made into more economically vibrant, equitable, and sustainable places.

References

Reference works are listed by chapter. Reference works for chapter 2 are subdivided by case study area.

CHAPTER 1

AAA Foundation for Traffic Safety. 2011. *Impact Speed and a Pedestrian's Risk of Severe Injury or Death*. Washington, D.C.: AAA Foundation. https://www.aaafoundation.org/sites/default/files/2011Pedestrian-RiskVsSpeed.pdf.

American Community Survey Reports. 2014. *Modes Less Traveled—Bicycling and Walking to Work in the United States: 2008–2012*. Washington, D.C.: U.S. Census Bureau. www.census.gov/prod/2014pubs/acs-25.pdf.

Brownson, Ross C., Tegan K. Boehmer, and Douglas A. Luke. 2005. "Declining Rates of Physical Activity in the United States: What Are the Contributors?" *Annual Review of Public Health* 26:421–43.

Federal Highway Administration. 1987. *Investigation of Exposure-Based Pedestrian Accident Areas: Cross-walks, Sidewalks, Local Streets, and Major Arterials*. Publication No. FHWA/RD87-038. Washington, D.C.: Federal Highway Administration.

National Center for Safe Routes to School. 2015. "The Decline of Walking and Bicycling." *Safe Routes to School Online Guide*. http://guide.saferoutesinfo.org/introduction/the_decline_of_walking_and_bicycling.cfm.

Spoon, Chad. 2016. "Infographic: Run Errands on Foot or Bike—A Remedy for Adult Activity." *Move!* (blog), *Active Living Research*, April 14. http://activelivingresearch.org/ActiveTravelinfographic.

Urban Land Institute. 2015. *America in 2015: A ULI Survey of Views on Housing, Transportation, and Community*. Washington, D.C.: Urban Land Institute.

CHAPTER 2

Arlington

Arlington County Government. 2015. *Columbia Pike Neighborhoods Special Revitalization District Form Based Code*. Arlington County Government. https://arlingtonva.s3.amazonaws.com/wp-content/uploads/sites/31/2014/06/6_Attachments.pdf.

———. 2016a. "Columbia Pike Development History." Arlington County Government. http://projects.arlingtonva.us/neighborhoods/columbia-pike-development-history.

———. 2016b. "Columbia Pike Form Based Codes." Arlington County Government. http://projects.arlingtonva.us/neighborhoods/columbia-pike-form-based-codes/.

———. 2016c. "Columbia Pike Planning at a Glance." Arlington County Government. https://projects.arlingtonva.us/neighborhoods/columbia-pike-planning/.

———. 2016d. "Financial Tools." Arlington County Government. http://housing.arlingtonva.us/development/financial-tools/.

———. 2016e. "Housing on Columbia Pike." Arlington County Government. http://housing.arlingtonva.us/housing-columbia-pike.

———. 2016f. "Land Use and Zoning Tools." Arlington County Government. https://housing.arlingtonva.us/development/land-use-zoning-tools/.

Shaver, Les. 2014. "Pike Dreams." *Arlington Magazine* (July–August). www.arlingtonmagazine.com/July-August-2014/Pike-Dreams.

Shoreline

City of Shoreline. 2014. "Metro Transit RapidRide E Line Service Begins in February." Press release, January 27. City of Shoreline. www.shorelinewa.gov/Home/Components/News/News/1611/21.

———. 2016a. "Aurora Corridor Project." City of Shoreline. www.shorelinewa.gov/government/departments/public-works/capital-improvement-plan/aurora-corridor-project.

———. 2016b. "Aurora Corridor Project, N 145th–N 165th Streets." City of Shoreline. www.shorelinewa.gov/government/departments/public-works/capital-improvement-plan/aurora-corridor-project/aurora-corridor-project-n-145th-n-165th-streets.

———. 2016c. "Aurora Corridor Project, N 165th to N 205th Streets." City of Shoreline. www.shorelinewa.gov/government/departments/public-works/capital-improvement-plan/aurora-corridor-project/aurora-corridor-project-n-165th-to-n-205th-streets.

———. 2016d. "Construction: Aurora Corridor N 192nd to N 205th." City of Shoreline. www.shorelinewa.gov/government/departments/public-works/capital-improvement-plan/aurora-corridor-project/construction-aurora-corridor-n-192nd-to-n-205th.

City of Shoreline Aurora Corridor. 2011a. "Rain Garden Plaza at N 192nd Street." City of Shoreline. www.shorelinewa.gov/home/showdocument?id=8441.

———. 2011b. "Retaining Walls and Green Screens." City of Shoreline. www.shorelinewa.gov/home/showdocument?id=8608.

———. 2014. "What Is the Aurora Corridor Project?" City of Shoreline. www.shorelinewa.gov/home/showdocument?id=8426.

Economic Development Council of Seattle and King County. 2014. "City of Shoreline: A Renaissance on Aurora Avenue." *Shoreline Area News*, April 11. www.shorelineareanews.com/2014/04/city-of-shoreline-renaissance-on-aurora.html.

King County. 2016. "About Metro." King County. http://kingcounty.gov/depts/transportation/metro/about.aspx.

King County Metro. 2014. *RapidRide E Line*. Seattle, WA: King County Government. www.kingcounty.gov/transportation/kcdot/MetroTransit/RapidRide/~/media/transportation/kcdot/MetroTransit/RapidRide/E_Line_handout_201402.ashx.

———. 2016. "More Frequent, Reliable Bus Service Will Soon Connect More Riders to Congestion-Free Light Rail." *Metro Matters* (blog), March 9. King County Metro. https://metrofutureblog.wordpress.com/2016/03/09/more-frequent-reliable-bus-service-will-soon-connect-more-riders-to-congestion-free-light-rail.

Lindblom, Mike. 2014. "RapidRide Use Is Way Up." *Seattle Times*, July 7. http://www.seattletimes.com/news/rapidride-use-is-way-up/.

Puget Sound Regional Council. 2016. "Frequently Asked Questions." Accessed September 6. www.psrc.org/about/faq.

Urban Land Institute. 2012. *Shifting Suburbs: Reinventing Infrastructure for Compact Development*. Washington, D.C.: Urban Land Institute. http://uli.org/wp-content/uploads/ULI-Documents/Shifting-Suburbs.pdf.

Cleveland

Cleveland Historical. 2016. "Millionaires' Row." *Stories*. Center for Public History. Accessed September 6. http://clevelandhistorical.org/items/show/10.

Greater Cleveland Regional Transit Authority. 2012a. "HealthLine." Greater Cleveland Regional Transit Authority. www.riderta.com/routes/healthline.

———. 2012b. "RTA's HealthLine—the World-Class Standard for BRT Service." Greater Cleveland Regional Transit Authority. www.riderta.com/healthline/about.

———. 2015. "Transit System Developments." Presentation given at the Ohio Transportation Engineering Conference, Columbus, OH, October 2015. https://www.dot.state.oh.us/engineering/OTEC/2015_OTEC_Presentations/Tuesday_Oct.27/43/OTEC%20RTA%20Overview%20E%2079%20and%20Red%20Line%20HealthLine%20Ext%209-30-15.pdf.

Hellendrung, Jason. 2012. "HealthLine Drives Growth in Cleveland." *Urban Land Magazine,* July 13. http://urbanland.uli.org/economy-markets-trends/healthline-drives-growth-in-cleveland/.

Miller, Jay. 2012. "HealthLine Serves as Catalyst: Economic Development along Euclid Follows Debut of Hybrid Transit." *Crain's Cleveland Business*, October 29. www.crainscleveland.com/article/20121029/EUCLIDARTICLES/310299988/healthline-serves-as-catalyst.

Partnership for Sustainable Communities. 2012. *Transit as Transformation: The Euclid Corridor in Cleveland*. Washington, D.C.: Partnership for Sustainable Communities. https://www.sustainablecommunities.gov/sites/sustainablecommunities.gov/files/docs/cleveland-euclid-corridor.pdf.

RTA HealthLine. 2016a. "Goals." RTA HealthLine. Accessed September 6. www.rtahealthline.com/project-overview-goals.asp.

———. 2016b. "History." RTA HealthLine. Accessed September 6. www.rtahealthline.com/project-over-view-history.asp.

———. 2016c. "What It Is—Vehicle Information." RTA HealthLine. Accessed September 6. www.rtahealthline.com/healthline-what-is-vehicle.asp.

———. 2016d. "Where It Goes." RTA HealthLine. Accessed September 6. www.rtahealthline.com/healthline-where-goes.asp.

———. 2016e. "Who It helps." RTA HealthLine. Accessed September 6. www.rtahealthline.com/healthline-who-helps.asp.

Columbus

Duffy, Jamie. 2012. "In Columbus, Ohio, an Arts Belt Is Thriving." *New York Times*, August 7. www.nytimes.com/2012/08/08/realestate/commercial/in-columbus-ohio-the-short-north-arts-belt-is-thriving.html.

Evans, Walker. 2013. "Pandora Tackles Parking, Shopping and Other Short North Issues." *Columbus Underground,* October 21. www.columbusunderground.com/pandora-tackles-short-north-parking-shopping-arts-and-other-neighborhood-issues.

Hambrick, Jennifer. 2010. "A Brighter Future Begins Now: Dream Job Delights Newly Appointed SNBA Director." *Short North Gazette,* March 2010. www.shortnorth.com/Menges.html.

HighBall Columbus. 2016. "The History of HighBall." Highball Columbus. Accessed September 6. http://highballcolumbus.org/about/.

Ohio Secretary of State. 2016. "Corporation Details: The Short North Business Association." Jon Husted, Ohio Secretary of State. Accessed September 6. www5.sos.state.oh.us/ords/f?p=100:7:0::NO:7:P7_CHARTER_NUM:612525.

Short North Arts District. 2015a. "About." Short North Alliance. http://shortnorth.org/about/.

———. 2015b. *Short North Arts District 2015 Annual Report*. Columbus, OH: Short North Alliance. http://shortnorth.org/wp-content/uploads/2015/02/2015_SNA_annual_report_final_1_29.pdf.

———. 2016a. "Community Festival." Short North Alliance. http://shortnorth.org/events/community-festival/.

———. 2016b. "History." Short North Alliance. http://shortnorth.org/see-experience/history/.

Short North Gazette. 2016. "Short North Organizations." *Short North Gazette.* Accessed September 6. www.shortnorth.com/ShortNorthOrganizations.html.

Stonewall Columbus Inc. 2016. "Stonewall Columbus Pride Parade." Stonewall Columbus Inc. https://www.columbuspride.org/parade.

Orlando

Arms, Jeffrey. 2015. "Edgewater Drive: Living through the Road Diet and Celebrating 13 Years as a Complete Street." In *Complete Streets: Implementation Projects from Vision to Reality*. Presentation given at the American Planning Association Florida Conference, Hollywood, FL, September 9. www.floridaplanning.org/wp-content/uploads/2015/09/CompleteStreets-Implementation-Henry-Sniezek-Jeffrey-Arms-Peter-Gies-Scott-Brunner-Steve-Braun-Teresa-Lamar-Sarno.pdf.

College Park Neighborhood Association. 2012. "History." College Park Neighborhood Association. http://mycpna.org/history.

Federal Highway Administration. 2001. "Edgewater Drive Before and After Re-Striping Results." U.S. Department of Transportation, Federal Highway Administration. http://contextsensitivesolutions.org/content/case_studies/edgewater-drive/.

Project for Public Spaces. 2016. "Edgewater Drive: Improving Safety and Supporting a Main Street." Project for Public Spaces. Accessed September 6. www.pps.org/reference/rightsizing-edgewater-drive-in-orlando-florida-for-safety-gains-and-to-promote-alternative-transportation/.

Smart Growth America National Complete Streets Coalition. 2015. *Safer Streets, Stronger Economies: Complete Streets Project Outcomes from across the Country*. Washington, D.C.: Smart Growth America. www.smartgrowthamerica.org/documents/safer-streets-stronger-economies.pdf

Rochester

Bonestroo. 2009. *Rochester 2nd Street Corridor Framework Plan*. St. Paul, MN: Bonestroo. www.rochestermn.gov/home/showdocument?id=4724.

Grossfield, Edie. 2014. "New 'Uptown' Area Shaping Up." *Post-Bulletin,* April 10. www.postbulletin.com/news/local/new-uptown-area-shaping-up/article_681fd943-4822-528c-b0f1-49aee73dca81.html.

Kiger, Jeff. 2013. "Construction Builds Concerns." *Post-Bulletin*, July 20–21. www.postbulletin.com/content/tncms/assets/v3/eedition/b/47/b473b1cb-a0bf-57da-b109-80073df0de40/51eaa27a2d6bf.pdf

CHAPTER 3

Schildt, Chris, and Victor Rubin. 2015. *Leveraging Anchor Institutions for Economic Inclusion*. Sustainable Community Series. Oakland, CA: PolicyLink. www.policylink.org/sites/default/files/pl_brief_anchor_012315_a.pdf.

Tennessee Department of Transportation. 2016. "Corridor Management Agreements." Tennessee State Government. Accessed September 6. https://www.tn.gov/tdot/article/tdot-long-range-planning-division-corridor-management-agreements.

CHAPTER 4

PwC and the Urban Land Institute. 2015. *Emerging Trends in Real Estate® 2016*. Washington, D.C.: PwC and the Urban Land Institute. http://uli.org/research/centers-initiatives/center-for-capital-markets/emerging-trends-in-real-estate/americas/.

Acknowledgments

The Building Healthy Places Initiative and the Rose Center for Public Leadership are grateful for the generous support of the **Robert Wood Johnson Foundation**, the **Colorado Health Foundation**, and the **ULI Foundation**.

We also gratefully acknowledge the contributions of the following people to this report:

Reviewers

Clare De Briere
Chief Operating Officer and Executive Vice President, the Ratkovich Company
Los Angeles, California

James Moore
Principal, Jacobs Advance Planning Group
Tampa, Florida

Sharon Roerty
Senior Program Officer, Robert Wood Johnson Foundation
Princeton, New Jersey

Christopher Smith
Senior Program Officer, Colorado Health Foundation
Denver, Colorado

Bob Taunton
President, Taunton Group LLC
Boise, Idaho

Healthy Corridors National Working Group Members

Patricia Clare
Senior Planner, Neel-Schaffer
Louisville, Kentucky

Clare De Briere
Chief Operating Officer and Executive Vice President, the Ratkovich Company
Los Angeles, California

Skye Duncan
Director, Global Designing Cities Initiative, National Association of City Transportation Officials (NACTO)
New York, New York

Dan Eernissee
Economic Development Manager, City of Shoreline
Shoreline, Washington

Aliza Gallo
Economic Development Manager, City of Oakland
Oakland, California

Stuart Levin
Physician, Wake Internal Medicine Consultants
President, Blue Ridge Corridor Alliance
Raleigh, North Carolina

Brandon McGee
State Representative, State of Connecticut
Hartford, Connecticut

Ed McMahon
Senior Resident Fellow, Urban Land Institute
Washington, D.C.

James Moore
Principal, Jacobs Advance Planning Group
Tampa, Florida

Jim Murley
Chief Resilience Officer, Miami-Dade County
Miami, Florida

Khanh Nguyen
Portfolio Director, Healthy Living, Colorado Health Foundation
Denver, Colorado

Alysia Osborne
Director of Historic West End, Charlotte City Center Partners
Charlotte, North Carolina

Matthew Roe
Director, Designing Cities Initiative, National Association of City Transportation Officials (NACTO)
New York, New York

Ken Schwartz
Senior Vice President, Planning Services, Vanasse Hangen Brustlin Inc. (VHB)
Watertown, Massachusetts

Christopher Smith
Senior Program Officer, Colorado Health Foundation
Denver, Colorado

Gary Toth
Senior Director, Transportation Initiatives, Project for Public Spaces
Lambertville, New Jersey

Matthew Trowbridge
Associate Professor, University of Virginia School of Medicine
Charlottesville, Virginia

Michael Wojcik
City Council Member, City of Rochester
Rochester, Minnesota

Denver—Federal Boulevard Local Leadership Group

Dave Thorpe (Chair)
Managing Director, Design & Construction, Silverwest Hotels
Denver, Colorado

J.J. Folsom
Senior Associate, Progressive Urban Management Associates (P.U.M.A.)
Denver, Colorado

Joe Knopinski
Managing Principal, Development Planning and Financing Group Inc. (DPFG)
Denver, Colorado

Brice Leconte
Founder, iUnit
Denver, Colorado

Sheila Lynch
Land Use Program Coordinator, Tri-County Health Department
Greenwood Village, Colorado

Susan Powers
President, Urban Ventures LLC
Denver, Colorado

Josh Radoff
Principal, YR&G
Denver, Colorado

Jay Renkens
Director of Denver Operations, MIG
Denver, Colorado

Sandi Thomas
Vice President and General Manager Denver Division, Newland Communities
Centennial, Colorado

Cate Townley
Built Environment Specialist, Colorado Department of Public Health and Environment
Denver, Colorado

Beth Vogelsang
Principal and Owner, OV Consulting
Golden, Colorado

Boise—Vista Avenue Local Leadership Group

Bob Taunton
President, Taunton Group LLC
Boise, Idaho

Mary Andrews
Former Director of Economic Development, Boise State University
Boise, Idaho

Cece Gassner
Director of Economic Development, Boise State University
Boise, Idaho

AnaMarie Guiles
Director of Housing and Community Development, City of Boise
Boise, Idaho

Jim Hansen
Commissioner, Ada County Highway District
Boise, Idaho

Dave Kangas
President
Vista Neighborhood Association
Boise, Idaho

Rebecca Lemmons
Director of Community Impact, United Way of Treasure Valley
Boise, Idaho

Ben Quintana
Council Member, City of Boise
Organizational Development Program Manager, St. Luke's Health System
Boise, Idaho

Los Angeles—Van Nuys Boulevard Local Leadership Group

Melani Smith (Chair)
Urban Planning Consultant,
NextPhase LA
Los Angeles, California

Jean Armbruster
PLACE Program Director, Los Angeles County Department of Public Health
Los Angeles, California

Michael Banner
President and CEO, Los Angeles LDC Inc.
Los Angeles, California

Jane Blumenfeld
Former Acting Deputy Director, Los Angeles Department of City Planning
Los Angeles, California

Nat Gale
Principal Project Coordinator, Los Angeles Department of Transportation
Los Angeles, California

Diane Philibosian
Director, Institute for Community Health and Wellbeing, California State University at Northridge
Los Angeles, California

Dan Rosenfeld
Vice President, Indivest Inc.
Los Angeles, California

Carter Rubin
Great Streets Program Manager, Office of Mayor Eric Garcetti
Los Angeles, California

Susan Wong
Legislative Deputy for Felipe Fuentes, Los Angeles City Councilmember for CD7
Los Angeles, California

Nashville—Charlotte Avenue Local Leadership Group

Ryan Doyle (Chair)
General Manager, oneC1TY
Nashville, Tennessee

Ted Cornelius
Vice President of Health Innovation, YMCA of Middle Tennessee
Nashville, Tennessee

Laurel Creech
Former Chief Service Officer, Nashville Mayor's Office
Nashville, Tennessee

Mark Deutschmann
CEO, Village Real Estate
Nashville, Tennessee

Kim Hawkins
Principal, Hawkins Partners Inc.
Nashville, Tennessee

Tracy Kane
Attorney, Dodson, Parker, Behm & Capparella PC
Nashville, Tennessee

Dana Neal
Director of Business Development, Skanska
Nashville, Tennessee

Bill Paul
Director, Metro Nashville Public Health Department
Nashville, Tennessee

Cyril Stewart
President, Cyril Stewart LLC
Nashville, Tennessee

Alan Thompson
Vice President, Ragan-Smith Associates
Nashville, Tennessee

John Vick
Epidemiologist, Metro Nashville Public Health Department
Nashville, Tennessee

Participants in Healthy Corridor Forums and Study Visits

Karen Abrams
Community Relations Manager, Pittsburgh Urban Redevelopment Authority
Pittsburgh, Pennsylvania

David Bailey
Principal, Hastings Architecture Associates
Nashville, Tennessee

Jamie Bussel
Program Officer, Robert Wood Johnson Foundation
Princeton, New Jersey

Ray Gastil
Planning Director, City of Pittsburgh
Pittsburgh, Pennsylvania

Mike Higbee Jr.
President, Development Concepts Inc.
Indianapolis, Indiana

Gregory Hunter
Director, Cushman and Wakefield
Oakland, California

Ed Icenogle
Senior Shareholder, Icenogle Seaver
Pogue PC
Denver, Colorado

Robin-Eve Jasper
President, NoMa Business Improvement
District
Washington, D.C.

Mike Kromrey
Executive Director, Together Colorado
Denver, Colorado

Michelle Larkin
Associate Vice President, Robert Wood
Johnson Foundation
Princeton, New Jersey

Bert Mathews
President, the Mathews Company
Nashville, Tennessee

Gretchen Milliken
Director, Advanced Planning, Louisville Metro
Government
Louisville, Kentucky

Abel Montoya
Director, Long Range Strategic Planning,
Adams County
Brighton, Colorado

Alison Nemirow
Senior Associate, Strategic Economics
Berkeley, California

Danny Pleasant
Transportation Director, City of Charlotte
Charlotte, North Carolina

Sharon Roerty
Senior Program Officer, Robert Wood
Johnson Foundation
Princeton, New Jersey

Anwar Saleem
Executive Director, H Street Main Street Inc.
Washington, D.C.

Deanna Santana
City Manager, City of Sunnyvale
Sunnyvale, California

Amy Slonim
Senior Program Officer, Robert Wood
Johnson Foundation
Bellingham, Washington

Olga Stella
Executive Director, Detroit Creative Corridor
Center
Detroit, Michigan

Adam Theis
Assistant Vice President for Capital Planning,
Indiana University
Bloomington, Indiana

Mary Ellen Wiederwohl
Chief, Louisville Forward, Louisville Metro
Government
Louisville, Kentucky

Marja Winters
Assistant City Manager, City of Benton
Harbor
Benton Harbor, Michigan

A special thank you goes to all stakeholders
who participated in local workshops and
study visits in each of the four demonstration
corridors, including residents, community
advocates, public health professionals, public
sector leaders, designers, investors, and
developers.

BACK COVER IMAGES, CLOCKWISE FROM TOP:
Bus infrastructure, such as shelters, can provide safe, shaded, and dry places for passengers to
wait for transit. *(Craig Kuhner)* | Clearly marked bike lanes should be incorporated where ap-
propriate. *(Craig Kuhner)* | Activated street edges, including murals and windows into adjacent
developments, can increase pedestrian activity and street life. *(Bailey Lytle, Short North Alliance)*